Ask Grandma?

CYNTHIA CARICHE' CARTER

TO CONTACT CYNTHIA CARICHE' CARTER
Visit AskGrandmaBook.com, or send an e-mail to
Grandma.Cariche@gmail.com

My Prayer

Thank you Father God for the completion of my book.
It was your love, mercy, grace and spirit that made it all
possible.
You put your words in my heart and mind.
I give you all the honour and glory, knowing I was the
instrument used for the purpose.

Thank you Again,
Your Humble Servant
Grandma
Cynthia Cariche' Carter

Revelation

Jeremiah was the name of the person God used, "An Angel in Disguise". His name was Jeremiah Paschal, because of his name being biblical and a book in the bible, I knew God had a message for me. I searched the book of Jeremiah, chapter by chapter and verse by verse until I came upon Chapter 30 verses 1 and 2.

This is what I read.

[1]The word that came to Jeremiah from the Lord, saying, [2]Thus speaketh the Lord God of Israel, saying, write thee all the words that I have spoken unto thee in a book.

2 Timothy Chapter 1 Verse 5

When I call to remembrance the unfeigned faith that is in thee, which dwelt first in thy grandmother Lois, and thy mother Eunice; and I am persuaded that in thee also.

Dr. Eugene G. Sherman

Contents

Preface

The traditional human family consists of Father, Mother, and at least one child, that configuration is known as the nuclear family. In those instances where a grandparent is living with the family, the unit is known as an extended family. There are many values in the extended family setting. The extended family members, three generations is referred to as Grandfather or Grandmother, generally that person is the grandmother owing to longevity her presence in the family provides invaluable opportunities for both the parent and the children. She is a source of assistance with the household chores but her knowledge and past experiences are invaluable, in the training of children. In this connection the children are frequently prone to ask Grandma.

This book is a collection of Topics that children specifically and adults in general may well seek answers.

Hence, they Ask Grandma?

By Dr. Eugene G. Sherman

Dedication

I dedicate this book to all Grandmothers with love.

Especially my Grandmother
Carrie Walker Hunter

My two Loving Aunts
Rose R Johnson (Granny)
Addie Quaintance

My Daughter
Teresa Ann Larkin
and
My Granddaughter
Colette Cariche' Duncan

Acknowledgements

God is the first and most important (source) in my life. Ola Abdullah Thank you for your vision to write in the Southwest Georgia Paper.

Mr. Charles McNeil and Southwest Georgian Staff: Erica Cook and Shukinla Daniels thank you for your encouragement and help.

My friends Rita and Johnny Whitaker who walked, talked, listened, and prayed with me.

Ernestine and Alfred Greenlee my first Albanian friends who I wrote about in some of my articles.

Claudia Atkins, my glamorous friend, who always read my articles and passed them on to her friend's mother who enjoyed reading them.

Quen Carter – My one and only sister as she says we're Daddies Girls. Richard Hunter Jr.

Barbara Johnson and Alice Cole – My loving sisters/cousins who kept me in touch with family.

David L. Walker – The cousin I love he's been very instrumental in my life. Irving Carter- My Friend Forever.

Mrs. Irish Pickney – Thank you for encouraging me with positive feedback. We worked and retired together from school #20 in Paterson, N.J.

Lorenzo Hansford – We grew up together, He wrote me on several occasions and brought back memories of our childhood. The old church touched him.

Anita Ellen Young – "My Cyn" she calls me. I have always given words of encouragement to her. Now she's giving them to me.

Carl Ellen – Thank you for the letter note of encouragement. John McCormick Sr. - You're special Bo.

Mary Theadford – My Longtime Pennsylvania friend who shared my writings with her friends.

Alice D. Milton – Queen Mother of the Glamorous Red Rubies Red Hatters of Albany and Sylvester Georgia made me feel so special about my writings.

Janet Mitchell – My North Carolina friend gave me words of encouragement.

Emma Kate Holloway – My friend from Dawson, Georgia who admired my writing from the beginning would call and tell me the one's she enjoyed most.

Winston Gitters – Adopted family member, who helped made this journey possible.

Diane Williams – My college friend who encouraged me to stay in college.

Linda Sutton Hawkins – Sent a word of Love and Thanks.

Lillie Williams – Grandmother Friend who enjoys the articles.

Mr. J. Belk – Thanks for the name Grandma.

Thanks to the rest of my family and friends Vivian Johnson (God daughter), Ericka Johnson (Niece), Bernadette Morman (God daughter), Hattie Alston, Kathleen Wells, Floyd Johnson, Donald Thomas, Coretta Lawrence, Millie and Ace Elridge, Diane Cook, Jade Kessel, Calvin Johnson, Carmen Crislow, Doris Carter, Alyssia L. Hightower, Gloria Walker Anderson, Wanda Murray, June Brown, Jeanne Carter 1999, Anthony Smith 2009.

May God Bless All of you, Grandma

Introduction: Who Is Grandma?

Grandma is the mother of your parents. She is the glue that holds the family together. The person parents go to for the helping hand, listening ear, or advice, also the person who lifts you up when others have pushed you down. Because of her love grandma spoils the little ones. Where no one else would want them but her. Remember Grandma has traveled where you're going and in most cases knows you better than you know yourself, keeping a watchful eye and praying for you all the time. That's why you should cherish and respect the advice that grandma gives, she's lived through the stage of life where you are and has experienced so many details, good times and bad times, the beginning and ending of situations and circumstances, no matter what it was, Grandma overcame. It made her wiser and stronger because she didn't give up. If you have a grandmother, please love and respect her, throw your arms around her and show her how you feel. That would be the best gift you could give her. Now on the other hand, there's another role some grandmothers play raising their grandchildren. Situations and circumstances have caused her to take the mother's role almost without a choice, because she wants to keep the children in the family. This is a hard role for some grandmothers because times have changed so drastically, it's a big difference in how she raised her children and raising children today. I'm proud to say I was raised the old fashion way. When I arrived in Albany, Georgia to live after many years living in New Jersey I knew that I had to change from a northern girl and become a southern girl. It was not hard for me to do, because I was raised by a Georgian grandmother. Carrie Walker Hunter and her brother Benjamin Walker left Macon, Georgia with their families to come north. They brought the southern lifestyle with them. I was raised the same as if I was in Georgia. The only difference was that I lived in a quaint town called Passaic, New Jersey. Many black families from Georgia also moved to this town. We were the Walker and Hunter families. My grandmother was Carrie Walker Hunter and my grandfather was Richard Hunter Sr. They had three children Addie, Rose, and Richard Jr (My father). In the town of Passaic, the nationalities were Italians, Jews, Blacks, Polish, and Dutch. Every one lived in their own communities. The Jewish people were the merchants owning most of the businesses. The Italians were store owners. We called them neighborhood stores because they would give us credit when we did not have enough money until payday. In the Italian neighborhood I could smell spaghetti sauce cooking and it smelled so good. Next to our apartment house was Union Baptist Church in which our families stayed all day on Sunday, this was not unusual during that time because church was a big part of our lives.

I came up in a time when children were mandated to respect the elders and not talk back. The children of this modern generation where technology has taken over do not respect their elders as they should. They look at older people as old people who do not know or understand what is happening today. Like I tell the youth that I speak to, I did not come in to this world as an adult. They should be looking and wanting advice. When I was young I wanted advice but no one would give it to me. They would tell you what to do without any questions asked, I always wondered why they never explained anything. I guess that is why my book means so much to me, to be able to share my wisdom, knowledge and experience with others. Living in the south has been a great experience for me. When I talk to my family and friends from up north they ask me how I like living in the south. My answer to them is " I love it". I know love is a strong word but that's how I feel. The people in the south ask "Why did you move to Albany?" Like I should have moved to Atlanta or somewhere else. I'm happy I retired here. I can appreciate living in a slower environment. The south gets extremely hot, whereas the north gets extremely cold. People from the south are very friendly; they smile and speak without even knowing you. On the other hand, people from the north will know you and not speak, frown and sometimes even turn their heads.

Children from the north will say "yeah" "yes" "no" and "huh"; while children from the south respond with "yes ma'am" and "no ma'am". Another thing I had to get used to hearing was "you doing okay?" or "you doing alright?" I thought something looked wrong with me, not knowing it was the same as a northern person asking "How are you?" Because of so much land in the south, you never have a parking problem. In the north you do, because it's overcrowded. I never saw so much land in all my life until I moved to Georgia. I remember when I was a very young girl, my grandmother would tell me about the cotton fields and how they use to pick cotton in the hot sun. At that time I pictured trees in the cotton field, not knowing there wasn't any, because I told her she should have picked cotton where the shade was. When I arrived in Georgia I saw my first cotton field. I had a flashback and a reality check. No wonder they moved up north, I thought to myself. Grandma got a job as a domestic worker and grandpa went in to the mill. That's what they called factories back in the day.

Grandma

Life's Learning's (Be Thankful)

I've learned in life, it doesn't take a lot of money or material things to be happy, even though money is a means of survival. But what it takes to be happy is to have a personal relationship with God, making him first and the center of your life. As life goes on, God will speak to you in all kinds of ways. Our purpose in life is to be used for God's glory, serving in some kind of way. Sometimes it only takes a kind word, a listening ear, a hug, a smile, or a helping hand. Money can't buy any of these. If given, it would mean so much to the person. The spirit of God is powerful and can travel from heart to heart without a spoken word. We must always pray and be thankful, taking nothing for granted. When you awake and can see, talk, hear, walk, eat, sleep, and be in your right mind, be thankful. Whatever you have, be thankful and continue to pray. When we pray, we commune with God. We can pray anytime and anywhere. Our mothers and grandmothers prayed for us before we knew how to pray for ourselves. When you pray and do not receive an answer right away, don't fret, be patient. Some of our prayers take longer to be answered or won't be answered because God has a better plan. You must believe and never doubt, because when your prayer is answered it will manifest, be ever so ready. Also, if your motives are wrong, your prayers can be hindered. God knows we have needs and we can trust him to meet our needs. I remember my grandmother prayed all the time, on and off her knees. She would say prayer changes things. He may not come when you want him too, but he's right on time. Grandmothers knew the power of prayer, and it will bring you through many hard times. Prayer is a necessity if you are in a relationship that needs mending. Ask God to help you of any bitterness, to repair those relationships by forgiving, or asking for forgiveness. Write down anything that you think you are putting ahead of God in your life, such as money, relationships, material goods, or a career. Give it to God to renew your love and commitment to him, spending time worshiping him and praying always. You will see a change in your life.

Grandma

Caregiver

When most of my family members needed a caregiver, I was very young and their illness didn't last that long. Most caregivers are family members, which are caring for their mothers, fathers, wives, husbands or children. They knew these family members when they were healthy and active and it's hard now to see them in the condition they are presently in. As a caregiver, you have increased the stress in your life. Each care giving situation can be different, depending on the stage of the disease. Your stress will increase or decrease, depending on how you perceive your circumstances. If you are caring for someone who has dementia, such as Alzheimer's disease, it is often more stressful than caring for someone with a physical limitation. My relative from up north, who is caring for her mother who has Alzheimer's, is having a hard time dealing with the situation. The mother is functional; she can shower and dress herself at present, but repeats everything and is afraid to be alone. The daughter has to spend a lot of time with her mother. She calls me often and I listen, so she can relieve some of her stress. I think about the things she tells me. In my opinion caring for an Alzheimer's person is hard because most caregivers are in denial of their present condition. They see their love ones more as they were before the disease started, especially when they remember some things very well. This confuses the caregiver into thinking the person is not in a bad state. Most family members do not have training in this area. They should seek support groups that share their same experiences. There are many sources of information which you can obtain from your doctor, library, medical associations, related to specific diseases, and your computer. It is also important to take care of yourself when you are a caregiver because it can be very emotional. You should make a long list of favorite activities that help restore you. Check and see if family members, friends, or some good neighbours would help you. There might even be a day care center or home care services available. You should check out all options that could be helpful to you. It will make you a better person and an even better caregiver.

Grandma

You Only Keep What You Give Away

Have you heard this expression before? I bet you have. Early one morning on my way to work I was listening to the radio and the speaker spoke those words, "that you only keep what you give away". I thought to myself, how could that be? If you give it away, how could you keep it? This was a mind puzzle to me. All of a sudden a light bulb came on. I realized that it was spiritual and whatever is in your heart is what you give away. If you have an abundance of love, no matter how much you give away to others, you keep it. That's why it is so important to protect your heart. All types of things can enter and that's what you give away. Many people are hateful and they do hateful things. They are giving their hate away but keeping it within. Unknowingly, after saying all this, please stop and examine yourself. Be honest and if it is not love, figure out ways to make it love. Many people can't love because they don't know how. God is love but if you don't have the love of God within, you cannot truly love. If you want it, find it, pray for it and get it. Only then will you be on the path for love. When love enters your heart, you will know it because you will feel good about yourself and the things you do for others. Hearing that expression, "you only keep what you give away", meant a lot to me after I figuring it out. There are no limits to love and it can be expressed in many ways. Be careful what you give away. That's really something to think about.

Grandma

Two Sides to a Story

Many of you have heard that there are 2 sides to a story. It doesn't matter who is right or who is wrong. What matters is solving the problem. No problem goes away on its own. If someone is not treating you in the manner that you wish to be treated, instead of complaining to others, communicate this to the person involved. They may be totally unaware of their actions. In some cases the person complaining might be expecting too much from the other and may be the one at fault. In any case, whatever action it takes to correct the problem should be done. Having a creative activity helps keep down the negativity in your life that can cause friction with other people. A creative activity is something that you like doing such as reading, writing, painting, knitting, cooking or anything that is fulfilling to you. Being creative brings about satisfaction and keeps you busy in thought. It helps you escape into your own personal world and to stay in your own life, which allows peace, happiness and contentment to the soul. Some creative activities develop into bigger and greater things while others remain small. It doesn't matter because both bring about soul satisfaction. Just remember that blaming someone else for a problem is only an easy way out and doesn't solve anything. Always look at the part that you play in a situation and listen to the whole story, not just one side, in order to get clarity. Remembering this will make your life a lot less complicated!

Grandma

Advice & Opinion

Advice is something we all have given to someone at one time or another. It is a personal opinion of what a person thinks should be done in a given situation. All opinions should be carefully examined before given. Family and friends are usually the ones who voice their opinions to others, because they feel they can. This is not always a wise thing to do, because your opinion, in the form of advice, might not be desired by the person whom you are giving it too. Age is an important factor. The young person may need the advise where as the older person in some cases know what they're doing and your opinion is not needed unless they ask for the advice. I never give advice or my opinion to others freely. That in reality is minding other folks business, and that we should not do. Everyone has their own concerns and will do things according to how they feel. Life is a process and every individual is on their own journey. Those of us who have been on this journey longer should show love and compassion to those who need it by helping them when we can. Mistakes are made, that's why pencils have erasers. Here's something I could never understand about some people. When they reach a certain age, living and doing well, they act as if life has always been that way for them. None of us is perfect. We all have situations going on. Instead of giving our opinion we should pray for one another because we don't know why people act or do things differently. Sometimes they don't know either, but there is a reason. Take a family of siblings, raised the same way, eating, sleeping and living in the same house but when they become adults may live a different lifestyle. There's many things people do we may not understand, but if we pray, one day we will understand.

Grandma

Anger

Kind words can soften an angry heart. You never know what is stored inside of you. Today we have to be careful what we say and how we say it. People are easily offended because of anger that is stored within. You didn't cause, it but your words or actions may have caused the anger to surface. If the words are not spoken in a kind manner, it can cause an emotional experience that can be very dangerous, causing the person to act out or do something that they will regret. If something is bothering you, talk to someone you can trust that will listen and help you solve your problems. God is a problem solver, as the old people used to say. He is a lawyer in the courtroom and a doctor in the sick room. Their sayings have come a long way. Now we understand because we are walking in their shoes. The baggage that is being carried through the years might go back as far as childhood. I was raised without a father by a loving grandmother but growing up I wished that I lived in a household with two parents. My grandmother was my mother and father. Her love sustained me and made me the woman I am today. I had someone that loved me, raised me and provided for me. As I look back and think about those days, I was truly blessed and didn't really know it then but I know it now. I have a story to tell about grandma's love. We can't go around being a victim because of the picture society has painted for us to live by. It pays to think before we act, and get rid of the excess baggage we are carrying around and we will see how much better we feel. The load is too heavy to continue to carry. We need to think about what we have instead of complaining about what we don't have. We are amongst the living and that in itself is a blessing. So be happy, live, laugh and love!

Grandma

Old Student Goes to School

I mentioned in one of my articles that I went to college in the later years of my life. So it's never too late to learn. Anyone else who has that desire to go to school later in life should go for it. It may seem a little awkward at first, just don't give up and before you know it you will be in the swing of things. Remember if the brain hasn't been used academically in a long time, it has to be reprogrammed. Sometimes we don't realize how smart we are because many of us were never told. Changing your attitude changes a lot of things. A positive attitude will bring out the best in you and attract better people and things to your life. There was a man who could not read but wanted to read the bible. He was a much older man that was determined to go to school. I admired him because he did not let anyone stand in the way of his desire to learn and read the bible. A lot of senior people think it's too late or have lost the desire to do a lot of things that would lift their spirits. Never be ashamed of what you don't know because it's never too late to learn. The best way to learn from others is to admit that you don't know what they are talking about and ask them to please explain. That is how I learned. A person that thinks they know everything only limits themselves to learning. Education comes in many forms and from many places- home, environment, schools, churches, work places, family and friends. All these contribute to our learning. Seniors, did you know that you can attend college free if you have a desire to go. Remember, it's never too late.

Grandma

A Child's Most Influential Teacher

A child's most Influential Teacher is the mother, grandmother or whoever is raising the children including Fathers. All subjects such as reading, writing, and math can be improved at home by the parents. Math might be difficult because of the new methods being taught. It might confuse the child if we don't explain our method the same as the teachers do at school. If the child is having a problem with math, talk with the teacher on how you can help your child at home to improve their math. Our next most important subject is reading, it is the key to learning. Reading alone is not enough. You must comprehend what you read. To comprehend is to know and understand what you have read. Close your eyes and make a mental picture that might help. Writing skills are almost deleted because of the computer. Penmanship was a course where you learned to form your letters in order to form words. Now the computer and cell phones have replaced a lot of our writing skills. Also, we have to recognize that children learn in different ways.

Here are some of the ways children learn:

Visual Learners: learn best where they can see what they're learning. Drawing a picture or diagram of what they're trying to learn will help them tremendously.

Auditory Learners: learn mainly through their ears, reading important lessons aloud. You should make up poems, rhymes, memory cues and repeat spelling words.

Kinesthetic Learners: learn through their bodies. They might have to move around while studying, standing up when reading and acting out a lesson. It appears they cannot sit still.? No matter what method a child uses, what is important is that they are learning and you are responsible for helping them to learn.

Grandma

Young Women's Group

I was speaking with a young woman concerning a group she belonged to. They meet once a week to discuss biblical questions. It reminded me of the group that I belonged to when I was living in New Jersey. Eight young women participated in this bible study by debating questions. We divided ourselves into 2 groups of 4. It was amazing what we learned too, where this type of study prepared us to answer questions for those who were seeking answers. Simple questions can sometimes be the hardest to answer. We did not answer questions in our own interpretation but used scripture only. As I continued to talk to the young lady she told me how she and the group enjoyed the questions discussed. She shared the questions with me and I answered them in my own words:

Question 1: Are you using the Gifts God gave you for his glory? **Answer:** Yes. I write articles in the Southwest Georgian paper, inspirational articles that lift the spirit of others, causing them to feel better about themselves.

Question 2: What fostered spiritual growth during your life? **Answer:** When my husband and I separated and divorced. It was then I realized the pain and hurt that human love can cause. Only God's love could mend a broken heart and restore life more abundantly. Praying and studying the bible was my source.

Question 3: Are there any habits in your life that you need to break or get under control? **Answer:** All my habits that I knew were not good for my welfare I corrected. It was hard but I did it. I knew in order to be obedient to God's word I had to change. Being true to thyself is the first step. Honesty goes a long way and will cause you to grow spiritually.

I thanked the young lady for sharing her group questions with me. It brought back memories. Now why don't you try answering the questions to see how far you've come?

Grandma

Prejudice

I often wondered why people are prejudiced when we are all born with the same anatomy. The only difference is the color of our skin, which should not matter, because no matter what race we belong to, we still do the same. Think about that, especially the people who view others as being different because of their skin color. Yes cultures, lifestyles and environment can cause us to think and act differently but it is not a reason for us not to love or care for one another. This world would be a better place if we would all soften our hearts. If God loves us why can't we love each other? We are not on this earth forever, but while we are here, we should love and be kind to one another. If there is someone you dislike ask yourself why, especially if the person hasn't done anything to you to cause you to dislike them. Could it be you are envious or jealous? In many cases that is the problem. Sometimes when we are jealous of someone it is because they have what you want or are doing something that you want to do. You may not realize that you feel that way, but if you dislike someone without a cause that is usually the reason. Being envious and jealous is dangerous and can cause unnecessary problems. We should never judge a person because of the color of their skin but look at the contents of their character. None of us had a choice at birth to decide what race we would be born into. Do some soul searching for the answers to why we are prejudice.

Grandma

Congratulations to All the Graduates

It doesn't matter whether you graduated from Pre-k, High school, college or a university. The main thing is that you graduated. You have finished a course of study and been given a diploma or paper that stated such. Now you are ready to move on. If you're a Pre-k you are starting a new beginning at a public or private school that will be the choice of your parents. Leaving your day care or head start school, you were the older boys and girls. Now entering public or private schools, you are the younger students. The upper class students seem so much bigger than you .Your first few days will be different but you will soon adjust to the new school and the new rules. It won't be hard to do because your old school prepared you for the transition.

The High School graduate is planning to attend a college, university or technical school to further their education. Some graduates know the course of study they want and some don't. Furthering your education is a plus. It can open doors of opportunity to obtain a good job or career. Since the world is so competitive these days, one must do their best to achieve their goals. Those who have completed their course of study can now look for employment. Keep a positive attitude and send out as many resumes and applications as you can. Follow up on the jobs you have applied for by calling or sending a little note acknowledging that you haven't heard from them and would like to know the status of the position. Having a contact at the job you are interested in can be helpful. The person on the inside can give you the information you need about the position you have applied for or another position that might be available .Remember not to overload your resume and to use words of description. One page should be sufficient. Correct references are very important. Be sure to ask the person if you may use them as a reference and that they will say positive things about you. That person can cost you the job. Be sure that the phone numbers and addresses are accurate so that the references can be reached when needed. Prior job history and duties on previous jobs should also be acknowledged. Former supervisors should be accurate. I know it seems like a lot of work searching for your new career but putting the work in will pay off in the long run. I wish the graduates the very best as they move on into their future.

Grandma

Talking About People

I always wondered why people like to meddle in other people's affairs or talk about them. It seems to me if you take care of your own business, you wouldn't have time to be concerned about someone else. Talking about people just isn't nice. If you can't say something kind or good about a person, you shouldn't say anything at all. We should always lift a person up, not tear them down. People who are busy doing good deeds for themselves don't have time to downgrade someone else. When I first started teaching, I remember someone telling me that they didn't know I was teaching. My response to them was that good news never travels and that is so true. When something bad happens, everyone knows about it, especially the street committee. Good news doesn't move that fast because people don't seem to repeat it like they do bad news. I think that hearing bad news to some people makes them seem superior. It makes them feel like they have a better life. What they don't realize is that we all get a turn at having bad things happen to us in our lifetime. I remember a person who thought they were better than I was had the nerve to ask me how I became a teacher. Even though I was an adult student, I was still able to achieve my goals. Many older adults were entering college when I started. I had to ask myself was I insane doing this. Carrying the heavy books caused me to have shoulder and back pain. I would fall asleep studying at home for tests and writing long term papers. I remember a professor asking me had I ever thought about writing because I expressed myself well. Nobody had ever said that to me because people don't usually pay attention to the good qualities you have but usually focus on the negative ones they can find. I became inspired by the good grades I was getting and began to be proud of myself. Attending college was one of the best things that happened to me. It allowed me to focus on myself instead of other people. It kept me busy enough to stay in my own life. It changed my way of thinking and led me to a better lifestyle. I believe when you concentrate on yourself you don't have time to talk about someone else. You become valuable to you. People that do gossip about others should realize that they are wasting valuable time and in the long run they are only hurting themselves.

Grandma

Never Say Never

How many times have you said you would never do something and end up doing it? Maybe you have not as many times but I bet at least once. Sometimes doing a "never say never" turns out to be a good thing and sometimes it may not, depending on what it is. Think about what you said you would never do. Did it bring a smile or a frown upon your face? If you smiled, it was a good never, if you frowned, well, it may not have been so good. My never was "I would never move south," and I didn't say it just once. I said it many times because the town I lived in, some friends and family members were starting to move south. When I said I would never move south, at that time I meant it because I did not have a pretty picture in my mind of what the south was. My grandmother told me stories about growing up in the south. I knew about the marches Rev. Martin Luther King made, the bus incident with Rosa Parks, and so many other things that happened in the south. That was reason enough for my decision to say I would never move south. Living in the north, I never heard anything good about the south, it was always something negative, so that caused me not to even think about moving to the south. A friend of mine, who originated from the south, moved back home, and they invited me to visit with my family. I accepted the invitation and started to visit during my school breaks. Naturally, when you visit everything appears nice, the more I visited, the more I liked what I saw. The pace here is slower making a peaceful environment, which was my first attraction. Next, was the nice and affordable housing, the north is very expensive and most of the housing is old because they have very little land to build on. The weather here is great. Thank God, no more snow and ice. Education, religion, and family are very important here. A college town is good to live in causing you not to travel far to get the education, and you can attend some of the college functions also. There are plenty of churches. It appears that every religion is well represented. This should make folks good folks, don't you think? No matter what size your family is, it is said a family that prays together, stays together. All that is good, just be careful when you say you never will do something because you might change your mind and do the never.

Grandma

A Best Friend

Who is your best friend? It should be you. It's nice to have others as your friend but as I said your best friend to you should be you. First, you must be true to yourself. You have a right to all your feelings, the painful ones as well as the good ones. To feel all you can feel is to be truly human. You're either for yourself or against yourself. It's sad to say that so many people are literally their own worst enemies. They choose to do things that make them feel bad instead of good. This causes us not to appreciate ourselves. We should be enjoying the experience of being in charge of our lives. We should also protect ourselves from the pretending friend, the one who says they're your friend isn't. You can tell them early or late in life by their changing personality. Today they're your friend, tomorrow they're not. Observe their actions and listen to what they say and how they say it and that will tell you a lot about them. True friends will remain the same today, tomorrow, and forever. If you're a friend to yourself, you should always treat yourself nice. Never do harmful things and blame others. Remember, it was your choice. You were not being your friend. Some people treat others better than they treat themselves. One of the first things our parents taught us was right from wrong. These were valuable teachings and should remain with us through life, no matter what age we are. You cannot make right wrong and wrong right. Today's world has confused so many people because of the right and wrong situations. Right is right, and wrong is wrong. We can pretend we don't know the difference, but we do know when we're not doing the right thing towards ourselves and others. We don't experience the peace that we should. Our inner voice convicts us of what we did. We should get on the right path with love and respect, treating ourselves and others the way we want to be treated, now that's a best friend.

Grandma

How to Make a Friend

I have said in a few of my articles that with so many people in the world, no one should be friendless. I was telling my neighbor about all the nice people I met since I moved to Albany, Georgia from New Jersey. She replied by saying that I knew more people here than her and she lived here all of her life. That surprised me and I needed to take a closer look at the reason why. I know many people would like to have some new friends but just don't know how to make them. I learned a long time ago that you must first be a friend to yourself. Bring out the positive qualities that you possess. Talk less and listen more. People are attracted to positive people. Complainers are a turnoff to most people. Talking about illnesses and problems all the time can be a drag and no one wants to constantly hear about it. No one is perfect and everyone has something they are dealing with. You may be surprised to learn that other people may have problems bigger than yours but they deal with them differently through prayer and they are doers of their faith .I have heard it said that if you "pray-don't worry" and if you "worry-don't pray!"

Church is a good place to meet new friends because you have a variety of people to pick from and many organizations you can join to become involved with other people. You can also volunteer at a facility. There is always a need for volunteers in hospitals, soup kitchens, schools, churches and government agencies. I meet a lot of people when I travel alone. Sitting next to someone on a bus train or plane and having a conversation with them until you reach your destination can turn into a lasting relationship. I have met many people that way. No matter what you do you can always find a new friend but whether or not you keep that friend is up to you!

Grandma

Visionary Person

You are probably asking yourself what is a visionary person. A visionary person is one who feels or sees things before they happen, almost like seeing into the future. This is definitely a gift from God. When I was growing up, I thought my visions were everyone else's visions. I didn't know that everyone did not see or feel what I saw or felt. I am grateful that I became a visionary person. Having this gift allows me to avoid a lot of problems by making the right choices. I can usually see the whole picture from the beginning to the end. Most people are limited in what they see. Think about yourself and whether you might be a visionary person. Some people's visions come in the form of a dream. Remember the Reverend Martin Luther King Jr. and how many people did not see his dream, but they hoped it would materialize.

Let's talk about the dream since we are celebrating the 50 year march on Washington which took place on August 28, 1963. There were 250,000 people that traveled from all over the country to Washington D.C. to participate in a mass rally on the steps of the Lincoln Memorial. Dr. Martin Luther King delivered the "I have a Dream" speech. That speech was his vision and it was deeply rooted in the American dream. Throughout his brief life, his words communicated his vision, passion and faith which demonstrated his gift to inspire others to follow him. His techniques that promoted peaceful demonstrations were pioneered by Mahatma Gandhi, whose belief was in the power of love and non-violence. Dr. King's last speech on April 3, 1968 in Memphis, Tennessee spoke about the difficult days ahead which didn't matter because he had been to the mountaintop and saw the promise land. He informed the people that one day they would get to the promise land. It appeared he had a vision that he wasn't going to live a long life. He talked about how he was happy and wasn't worried about anything and that he feared no man. Martin Luther King just wanted to do God's will and be remembered as a "drum major for justice" because his eyes had seen the glory of the coming of the Lord. He was assassinated the next day on April 4, 1968. Dr. King was a visionary person who saw into the future. Thank God that some things did change and that he was our drum major for justice. We all remember that he had a dream and we know that we are living it now, 50 years later.

Grandma

You Can Be Replaced

Doing too many things at one time is not good for the body, soul or mind. If you have too many irons in the fire as the old saying goes or doing too many things at one time, it is not good. Something is going to get neglected because it takes time to focus. You should organize and prioritize before taking on some of your task. Some task can be done at a later date by someone else or not at all. When we feel no one else can do what we do we're not thinking clearly and we are harming ourselves in a great way, especially our health because we are moving in a rapid pace. Remembering an incident that happens at work one Monday morning, I noticed everyone was quiet and not talking. The only thing said was that the head of management was coming to speak to us. Everyone was thinking the worse. He told us that our supervisor would no longer be with us because of what happened over the weekend. We were all shocked and saddened. Our past supervisor was a happy go lucky type of person. He told us about a wedding he was going to attend over the weekend. In fact it was his niece who was getting married. It was said that he was dancing with food in his mouth and choked to death. Nobody in the company could believe what we had heard, but had to accept it because it was true. After telling the sad story, our new supervisor was introduced to us. It was at that moment that I realized how fast we can be replaced. It was a wakeup call for me. I also realized that the world continues on, with or without me. I have shard this story with many people, especially those who think no one can do a job but them. Don't ever think you can't be replaced because you can. Just accept your responsibilities without overloading yourself and let others help you!

Grandma

Resume & Interview

To the young people who are looking for work, most job fairs or companies require you to send or give them a resume. It is very important to have a resume available. Your resume is your personal, educational and work history. The word resume is a French word meaning summary. That is what a resume does, summarizes facts about you. It has become a job hunting tool that is so often the deciding factor in determining whether or not you get an interview with the employer. A well prepared resume will provide important information for the conversation between the applicant and the prospective employer .After submitting your one page resume with cover letter, you should be notified for an interview. The purpose of the interview is to evaluate your personality, background and qualifications for the job you are seeking. You should dress appropriately when you go on an interview. If you don't know what to wear, ask someone to help you. Being well groomed and neat is very important because if you are hired you will be representing the company. You should be courteous and well poised and describe your experience skills and abilities precisely and accurately. Honesty is respected and you should be knowledgeable about the companies operation. Always let the interviewer lead with the questioning and only answer what is asked. Think before you answer and if you don't understand the question, politely ask the interviewer to repeat it. Don't give the answers you think the employer wants to hear but strive for honesty and consistency. Remember that the person interviewing you has skills in the area of hiring and already know the type of candidate they are looking for. You don't have to overplay your technical knowledge. The employer only wants to know who you are. If it becomes obvious that you are not the right person for the job you are applying for, ask them if there is another area that you might be qualified for. It shows them that you are really interested in the company. Always keep your resume ready and updated and it might get you the job. You never know when a good job becomes available.

Grandma

Where Are the Good Men?

That seems to be the complaint of some women today. It appears that there are less and less men around. There are many reasons and by now I know you know the reasons. It's been said we women outnumber the men, so this give the men a choice to be choosey or to have more than one woman. Not all men but some. I remember one day I asked one of my friends, who were a male the question, what was wrong with the men? He said "nothing, it's the women at fault because they allow the man to do the things they do and she accepts his behavior." Naturally I disagreed with him. He stated that all women like me do not accept undesirable behavior, but because there are so many women to pick from, he finds the one that accepts his behavior. Sorry to say some women will do anything to have a man, whereas others will not because she knows the type of man she desire and refuses to settle for less. Her experience motivates her to know what she desires in a man because it's hard to settle for less when you have or are making a comfortable life style for yourself. I think women are natural home makers. In most situations they know how to accomplish what they desire and if they find the right mate they could have a beautiful and complete life. To all the males who are looking for a good woman, she's out there looking for you; all ages are in search of a good man. The young women should be treated with love and respect, not used and abused. She should love and respect herself, allowing others to do the same. Remember she is learning so treat her with kindness so she can be a treasure to you. Now on the other hand, the older women have been married, divorced, or widowed and have experience on what a man is really like. Meaning she had a lot of experience and is ready and seasoned for the right man.

Grandma

Family Reunion

The purpose of family reunions is to see family members on a joyous occasion. Before we had family reunions, we would gather for funerals or weddings. That would usually be the only time families would assemble together. Weddings were invitational and every family member did not get invited. Funerals were for whoever wanted to come in or out of state on a short notice and from this sad occasion was the birth of family reunions. Family members decided to get together on a joyous occasion. I remember observing a family that started their reunion plans after the funeral. Captains were chosen from the heads of the families from each state. The captains were in charge of giving other family members information in their state. Then they organized a family council that would meet occasionally to plan the events that they wanted to participate in, set up a program and talk it over with other family members. The first thing they did was pick the date and time for the reunion.. That was very important to make it convenient for everyone to attend. A good reliable hotel that catered to reunions would be the next item on the agenda to be discussed. That would be important because a lot of time is spent at the hotel. After finalizing the reunion plans, information is sent out to family members who are on the list. It would include the cost and dates to respond.

You should always try to attend your family reunions because it is a time when young and old come together and spend valuable time with each other. This is especially informative for the younger generations who might never have known their grandmother, grandfather, aunts, uncles or cousins if they had not attended a reunion. Many lasting relationships have formed from these events. It also gives people the opportunity to visit a state that they have never been to before. It's good to get away even for a short period of time because it's not the quantity but the quality of the time spent. We never know from one year to the next what will happen so we should enjoy all that we can while we can!

Grandma

The Stroke

We often hear that someone we know had a stroke, but do we know what it is and what caused it? Many of us don't but would like to know. Doctors call it a cerebral emergency. Cerebral means brain; emergency means sudden, therefore a stroke is the sudden interruption of blood flow through the arteries in the neck to the brain. This stoppage can be caused by a blood clot or a rupture in the walls of the artery. Without blood, the brain gets no life sustaining oxygen. Without oxygen, the brain suffocates and precious cells are killed or seriously damaged. It only takes four to five minutes for irreversible damage to occur. If the affected cells happen to be the cells that control your left arm or your memory, then those functions become impaired. If to many of your brain cells die, I hate to say this but so will you. Strokes just don't happen, they occur in the arteries that have been damaged or strained through the years. In many instances deposits of cholesterol and other substances build upon the inner walls of your arteries causing them to narrow and inhibit the free flow of blood. This is called atherosclerosis or hardening of the arteries, and it is the main cause of strokes. High blood pressure can also damage arteries. The stress and strain of elevated pressures can cause them to be scarred, in elastic, and hard. Also, aging can weaken arteries. The results are arteries that are more vulnerable to a blood clot getting lodged between their walls and blocking supply. If this happens to one of the arteries feeding blood to the heart, you will have a heart attack. If this happens to the artery, leading to the brain, you will have a stroke. Severe headaches are major symptoms of an impending stroke. Strokes do not discriminate, anybody can have one. The best way to avoid artery clogging cholesterol is to reduce the amount of fats and saturated fat in your diet. You can do this by eating less red meat, avoiding lunch meat, high fat dairy products, fried foods, and also butter. Fruits and vegetables protect you against a stroke; they are loaded with mineral potassium. If you need potassium in your body, here are some of the foods you should eat that are high in potassium: potatoes, avocados, oranges, cantaloupe, tomatoes, artichokes, carrots, and mangos. There is so much information that you can get free by visiting your library, using your computer, and asking your doctor and there are also free health seminars given during the year.

Grandma

Health Seminar

One of the churches in Albany gave a Health Awareness Seminar. If you read the Southwest Georgian paper on a weekly basis, you will know the events that take place each week. The doctor that spoke was my doctor. He spoke on high blood pressure and diabetes. He told us that we should feel connected with our doctors, and to ask questions concerning our health. He spoke about the foods that we eat that contain a lot of sodium, and sodium is salt. He stated that frozen foods were a better choice. Canned foods were not good because of the sodium. He had many types of food on display, and all of them were high in sodium. In other words, we like or are addicted to the foods we shouldn't eat. He also told us to stop eating processed foods and eat fresh vegetables, fruits, rice, and fresh cuts of meat. All of that sounded good at the seminar, but once you're home, it's hard. Your refrigerator and cabinets are full of what you shouldn't eat. Now that I am more aware of the foods that I shouldn't eat, I will eat less of the wrong foods and more of the right foods. He spoke on diabetes, in which blood sugar levels are too high because the body can't make or approximately use insulin. Insulin is a hormone that helps the body use or store glucose. People with diabetes need to be vigilant about their blood pressure. Nearly two out three people with diabetes have high blood pressure. This doubles cardiovascular disease's risk which can lead to heart attack and stroke. People with both diseases are also more likely to develop nerve, kidney, and eye damage. Getting your blood pressure tested each time you see your doctor, and taking steps to keep it in check, can help prevent such health problems. If you have diabetes, doctors recommend keeping your blood pressure below 130/80. Healthy habits to manage blood pressure include: controlling weight, exercising regularly, eating a healthy, low salt diet, replace some of the meat in your diet with some of the vegetables and whole grains, replace deserts and snacks with fresh fruits. Compare food labels and choose alternatives that are lower in calories, fat, and sugar; such as non-fat milk instead of 2%, Use smaller plates to help shrink your portion sizes, and walk every chance you get. Small lifestyle changes can help you lose pounds and lower your risks for diabetes. Even a modern weight lost improves your blood glucose levels which are good news if you already have diabetes. Losing weight doesn't require radical changes. These simple strategies can help you lose weight and keep it off.

Grandma

Me-Time and a Day to Do Nothing

What a title, its self explanatory. That's what a lady said. She wished she had more me -time to do nothing but relax. As she was speaking I realized she liked what she was doing but had robbed herself of her me-time. I think when this happens, it's because we don't take time out for ourselves .it is important to set aside a little time just for you. Take in consideration that you are the only one that can give you me- time. Another lady said "I would just like a day to do nothing, I'm too busy involved into too many things. I would love to have a day just to do nothing". There are many people who have days doing nothing and wished they had things to do. I know a few people who feel the same way these 2 ladies do.

I read years ago or heard it somewhere that we spend half of our lives complicated it and the other half simplifying it. I thought about this and it's true, we spend a lot of time working hard to make a life for ourselves trying to succeed in every way we can. We enjoy the years of our success helping our family, friends and others causing people to depend on us. We become accustomed to our lifestyle and it's hard to change and simplify it. Just like we plan to reach our goal, we have to plan for a life that is less stressful. Planning is always important for anything we do. It causes us to think before applying and is flexible for changes. All we have to do is take time for ourselves like we give to others. It's simple, we complicate it.

Grandma

Leader-Follower-Individual

There are 3 types of people in the world- a leader, a follower and an individual. A leader is a take charge person, the one who usually runs the show. I have a friend that has all the characteristics of a leader. She is very active in many organizations and supplies them with a lot of information. She enjoys being a leader and representing the groups that she belongs to. A good leader should be willing to listen and respect the opinion and ideas of others, which is not always the case.

In order to lead, you must have followers. Followers usually blend in with the crowd and go along with whatever is going on. Sometimes they don't even know the circumstances involved because they are riding on someone else's ideas. Followers don't like change although they may complain or talk about a situation. They remain as followers because they refuse to change, but will always support their leader.

People that are considered to be individuals look, think and act differently. They voice their opinion openly and are not concerned with what other people think of them. Individuals usually stand out in the crowd and are sometimes misunderstood because they are different. Most of them are gifted and talented and are motivated by their own thoughts and ideas. They seek sources for information, instead of people. Individuals usually love learning embrace knowledge and like to share with others. They can lead as well as follow and are good observers, but prefer to be individuals. My question is, are you a leader, follower or an individual?

Grandma

Thank You, Mr. Jason Belk

Thank you and your staff for having the patience to help my granddaughter grow up. As a grandparent, I know that?it takes a lot of love, patience, and understanding to work with children. Sometimes the difficult child ends up being one of your favorites that also loves and respects you. So here again, I thank you, thank you, thank you.

I know there are many mothers, fathers, and grandparents who feel the same way about you as I do. I am thanking you for them also. When I first thought about thanking you, I was just going to give you a thank you card, but the thought came to mind to let others know what a special person you are, so I decided to give the message in the Southwest Georgian paper. In fact, we should have a special day to honor you; you are a father figure to many of our children. They will never forget you. Another thing, thank you for giving me the name Grandma, my granddaughter and everyone else calls me Mema and since you gave me that name, I used it for my article name, and now many people greet me saying "Hi Grandma" just like you did whenever I came to visit. One thing I can truly say is that I never had to worry about my granddaughter being in your care because I knew she was in a safe environment at the Boys & Girls Club. I know that place will always have a special place in my granddaughter's heart?and in my heart too. It was a part of the village that helps raise a child. You and your staff make this possible for many families in Albany, and I hope they appreciate you as much as we do. I send a special prayer that God continues to bless you and keep you for our children, you are the best.

Thank you again, Grandma

The Greatest Gift: Love (Charity)
1 Corinthians 13: 1-13

The Bible is the greatest book. It never changes. It's the same yesterday, today, and forever.

King James Version

¹Though I speak with tongues of men and of angels and have not charity, I am become as sounding brass, or a tinkling cymbal. ²And though I have the gift of Prophecy, and understand all mysteries, and all knowledge; and though I have all faith, so that I could remove mountains, and have not charity, I am nothing.

³And though I bestow all my goods to feed the poor, and though I give my body to be burned, and have not charity it prophet me nothing. ⁴Charity suffered long, and is kind; charity envieth not; charity vaunteth not itself, is not puffed up,

⁵Doth not behave itself unseemly, seeketh not her own, is not easily provoked, thinketh no evil; ⁶Rejoiceth not in iniquity, but rejoiceth in truth. ⁷Beareth all things, believeth all things, hopeth all things, and endureth all things.

⁸Charity never faileth: but whether there be prophecies, they shall fail; whether there be tongues, they shall cease; whether there be knowledge, it shall vanish away. ⁹For we know in part and we prophesy in part.

¹⁰But when that which is perfect is come, then that which is in part shall be done away ¹¹When I was a child I spake as a child, I understood as a child, I thought as a child; but when I became a man I put away childish things.

¹²For now we see through a glass, darkly; but then face to face; now I know in part; but then shall I know even as also I am known. ¹³And now abideth faith, hope, charity, these three; but the greatest of all is charity.

New Living Translation

¹If I could speak any language in Heaven or on Earth but didn't love others, I would only be making meaningless noise like a loud gong or a clanging cymbal. ²If I had the gift of prophecy and if I knew all the mysteries of the future and knew everything about everything, but didn't love others, what good would I be? And If I had the gift of faith so that I could speak to a mountain and make it move, without love I would be no good to anybody

³If I gave everything I have to the poor and even sacrificed my body, I could boast about it; but if I didn't love others I would be of no value whatsoever. ⁴Love is patient and kind. Love is not jealous or boastful or proud or rude.

⁵Love does not demand its own way, it is not irritable, and it keeps no record of when it has been wrong. ⁶It is never glad about injustice but rejoices whenever the truth wins out.

⁷Love never gives up, never loses faith, is always hopeful, and endures through every circumstance. ⁸Love will last forever, but prophecy and speaking an unknown language and special knowledge will all disappear.

⁹Now we know only a little, and even the gift of prophecy reveals little! ¹⁰But when the end comes, all these special gifts will disappear. ¹¹It's like this, when I was a child I spoke and thought and reasoned as a child does. But when I grew up I put away childish things.

[12]Now we see things imperfectly, as in a poor mirror but then we will see everything with perfect clarity. All that I know now is partial and incomplete, but then I will know everything completely just as God knows me now.

[13]There are three things that will endure: faith, hope, and love and the greatest of these is Love.

Grandma

The Whole Armor of God
Ephesians 6: 11-18

As the New Year begins, let's put on the whole armor of God.

King James Version

[11]Put on the whole armor of God that ye may be able to stand against the wiles of the devil. [12]For we wrestle not against the flesh and blood, but against principalities, against powers, against the rulers of the darkness of this world, against spiritual wickedness in high power,

[13]Wherefore take unto you the whole armor of God that ye may be able to withstand in the evil day, and having done all, to stand. [14]Stand there for, having your loins girt about with truth and having on the breast plate of righteousness.

[15]And your feet shod of the preparation of the gospel of peace. [16]Above all, taking the shield of faith, where with ye shall be able to quench all the fiery darts of the wicked. [17]And take the helmet of salvation, and the sword of the spirit, which is the word of God. [18]Praying always with all prayer and supplication in the spirit and watching there unto with all perseverance and supplication for all saints.

New Living Translation

[11]Put on all of God's armor, so that you will be able to stand firm against all strategies and tricks of the devil [12]For we are not fighting against people made of flesh and blood, but against the rulers and authorities of the unseen world, against those mighty powers of darkness who rule this world, and against wicked spirits in the heavenly realms

[13]Use every piece of God's armor to resist the enemy in the

time of evil, so that after the battle you will still be standing firm [14]Stand your ground putting on the sturdy belt of truth and the body armor of God's righteousness

[15]For shoes, put on the piece that comes from the good news, so that you will be fully prepared. [16]In every battle, you will need faith as your shield to stop the fiery arrows aimed at you by satin.

[17]Put on salvation as your helmet, and take the sword of the spirit, which is the word of God. [18]Pray at all times and on every occasion in the power of the Holy Spirit. Stay alert and be persistent in your prayers for all Christians everywhere.

Grandma

Delight in the Lord
Happy Easter!

Psalm 37: 1-11: King James Version

[1]Fret not thyself because of evil doers, neither be thy envious against the workers of iniquity [2]For thy shall soon be cut down like grass, and wither as green herb

[3]Trust in the Lord and do well; so shall thy dwell in the land, and verily thou shall be fed. [4]Delight thyself in the Lord; and he shall give thee the desires of thine heart

[5]Commit thy way unto the Lord; trust also in him and he shall bring it to pass. [6]And he shall bring forth thy righteousness as the light and thy judgment as the noon day.

[7]Trust in the Lord; and wait patiently for him. Fret not thyself because of him, who prospereth in his way, because of the man who bring wicked devices to pass [8]Cease from anger, and forsake wrath: fret not thyself in any wise to do evil.

[9]For evil doers shall be cut off: but those that wait upon the Lord, they shall inherit the earth. [10]For yet a little while, and the wicked shall not be: yay, thou shall diligently consider his place and it shall not be.

[11]But the meek shall inherit the earth; and shall delight themselves in the abundance of peace.

Psalms 37: 1-11: New Living Translation

[1]Don't worry about the wicked; don't envy those who do wrong. [2]For like grass, they shall fade away, like spring time flowers they soon wither [3]Trust in the Lord and do good, then you will live safely in the land and prosper. [4]Take delight in the

Lord and he will give you your heart's desires. ⁵Commit everything you do to the Lord, trust him and he will help you. ⁶He will make your innocence as clear as the dawn and the justice of your Coors will shine like the noon day son. ⁷Be still in the presence of the Lord, and wait patiently for himto act. Don't worry about evil people who prosper or Fret about their wicked schemes. ⁸Stop your anger, turn from your rage! Do not envy others, it only leads to harm ⁹For the wicked will be destroyed, but those who trust in the Lord will possess the land. ¹⁰In a little while the wicked will disappear, though you look for them they will be gone ¹¹Those that are gentle and lowly will possess the land. They will live in prosperous security.

Grandma

Love One Another

King James Version
I John Chapter 4 Verses 7-10 and 18-21

[7]Beloved, let us love one another: for love is of God; and everyone that loveth is born of God and knoweth God [8]He that loveth not knoweth not God; for God is love [9]In this was manifested the love of God toward us because that God sent his only begotten Son into the world that we might live through him

[10]Herein is love, not that we loved God, but that he loved us, and sent his son to be the propitiation for our sins [18]There is no fear in love; but perfect love casteth out fear because fear hath torment. He that feareth is not made perfect in love

[19]We love him because he first loved us [20]If a man say, I love God and hateth his brother, he is a liar; for he that loveth not his brother whom he hath seen, how can he love God whom he hath not seen? [21]And these commandments have we from him. That he who love God love his brother also.

New Living Translation
I John Chapter 4 Verses 7-10 and 18-21

[7]Dear Friends, let us continue to love one another. For love comes from God. Anyone who loves is born of God and knows God. [8]But anyone who does not love does not know God - For God is love

[9]God showed how much he loved us by sending his only son into the world so that we might have eternal life through him [10]This is real love it is not that we loved God but that he loved us and sent his son as a sacrifice to take away our sins.

[18]Such love has no fear because perfect love expels all fear. If we are afraid it is for fear of judgment, and this shows that his love has not been perfected in us [19]We love each other as a result of his loving us first.

[20]If someone says, "I love God" but hates a Christian brother or sister that person is a liar; for if we don't love people, we can see, how can we love God whom we have not seen? [21]And God himself has commanded that we must love not only him but our Christian brothers and sister too.

Grandma

The Reason for the Season
The Birth of Jesus

Matthew Chapter 1: 18-24

[18]Now the birth of Jesus Christ was on this wise: When as his mother Mary was espoused to Joseph, before they came together, she was found with child of the Holy Ghost. [19]Then Joseph her husband, being a just man, and not willing to make her a public example, was minded to put her away privately.

[20]But while he thought on these things, behold the angel of the lord appeared unto him in a dream, saying Joseph, thou son of David, fear not to take unto thee Mary thy wife, for that which is conceived in her is of the Holy Ghost.

[21]And she shall bring forth a son, and thou shall call his name JESUS for he shall save his people from their sins. [22]Now all this was done, that it might be fulfilled which was spoken of the Lord by the prophet saying,

[23]BEHOLD A VIRGIN SHALL BE WITH CHILD, AND SHALL BRING FORTH A SON, AND THEY SHALL CALL HIS NAME IMMANUEL - MAN, which being interpreted is, God with us. [24]Then Joseph being raised from sleep did as the angel of the Lord had bidden him and took unto him his wife.

New Living Translation Matthew Chapter 1: 18-24

[18]Now this is how Jesus the Messiah was born. His mother, Mary was engaged, was engaged to be married to Joseph. But while she was still a virgin, she became pregnant by the Holy Spirit. [19]Joseph, her fiancé being a just man, decided to break the engagement quietly, so as not to disgrace her publicly.

[20]As he considered this, he fell asleep and an angel of the lord appeared to him in a dream "Joseph son of David" the angel said," do not be afraid to go ahead with your marriage to Mary. For the child within her has been conceived by the Holy Spirit.

[21]And she will have a son and you are to name him Jesus, for he will save his people from their sins". [22]All of this happened to fulfill the Lord's message through his prophet. [23]"Look! The virgin will conceive a child! She will give birth to a son and he will be called Immanuel, (meaning God is with us)"

[24]When Joseph woke up, he did what the angel of the Lord commanded; He brought Mary home to be his wife.

Grandma

Happy Father's Day

Psalms 1: King James Version

[1]Blessed is the man that walketh not in the counsel of the ungodly, nor standeth in the way of sinners, nor sitteth in the seat of the scornful. [2]But his delight is in the law of the Lord; and in his law, doth he meditate day and night.

[3]And he shall be like a tree planted by the rivers of water, that bringeth forth his fruit in his season; his leaf also shall not wither; and whatsoever he doeth shall prosper. [4]The ungodly and not so, but I like the chaff which the wind driveth away.

[5]Therefore the ungodly shall not stand in the judgment, nor sinners in the congregation of the righteous. [6]For the Lord knoweth the way of the righteous; but the way of the ungodly shall perish.

Psalms 1: Living Translation

[1]Oh, the joys of those who do not follow the advice of the wicked will stand around with sinners or join in with scoffers. [2]But they delight in doing everything the Lord wants; day and night they think about his law.

[3]They are like trees planted along the river banks bearing fruit each season without fail. Their leaves never wither, and all they do, they prosper. [4]But this is not true of the wicked. They are like worthless chaff, scattered by the wind.

[5]They will be condemned at the time of judgment. Sinners will have no place among the Godly. [6]For the Lord watches over the path of the Godly, but the path of the wicked leads to destruction.

Grandma
Happy Father's Day to all the Fathers!

High Blood Pressure

This article is dedicated to all of us who have high blood pressure. You may not want to read about it, but if I can write it, then you can read it. Sometimes it pays to be reminded of our medical situation and how important it is to take our medicine. Just because we feel good and think we're doing okay, skipping and missing our treatment does not mean it will stay that way. Let's get on the ball and start taking better care of ourselves. High blood pressure means that our hearts are working harder than normal to pump blood, putting your arteries under considerable strain. 140/90 or above is considered high blood pressure and can leave the arteries scarred and harden, and it is also harder for your heart to pump enough blood and oxygen to the organs and tissues. When blood is forced to work harder than normal for months or years, the heart tends to enlarge and also a blood clot can become lodged in a narrowed coronary artery causing a heart attack. To prevent this, you should have your blood pressure checked frequently because you can have high blood pressure and not know it. People of all ages can be affected by high blood pressure. Unfortunately, high blood pressure is difficult to detect. There are no symptoms, no lumps, or no bruises that can tell you that you may possibly have high blood pressure. Many people don't even know they have it. A normal blood pressure is 120/80, the first number is your systolic pressure, the pressure created when your heart contracts to pump blood. The second number is your diastolic, created when your heart is filling up with blood for the next beat. The good news is that high blood pressure can be prevented and controlled. Salt is a major hidden ingredient in the most unexpected foods. Cured meats, which a lot of people love, such as bacon, hot dogs, and sausages are loaded with salts, also soups, and canned vegetables. You can avoid eating a lot of salt by reading the labels that features the word "sodium." The American Heart Assoc. advises that you look for labels stating that the food products are "low sodium" or have no salt added. Eating too much fast foods can be a fast way to increase your blood pressure, so if you can, eat less fast foods. It might be a cheap meal, but in the long run it's not a healthy one, whatever we do we should do it in moderation. Exercise can lower your pressure. Aerobic exercise and brisk walking at least 3 times a week for 30 to 60 minutes reduces the amount of blood pumping through your arteries, and also reducing the amount of salt in your blood. Whatever you do to help keep your blood pressure under control, don't do it alone. Get your family or friends involved. Go bike riding, take a walk, and buy foods that everyone else can eat. Making it a healthy lifestyle for them as it is for you.

Grandma

Age

We are moving into another year, which means we will all be adding another year to our lives. In other words, we will be a year older. When some people reach a certain age, they consider themselves as being "old". In my opinion, old is a state of mind. You've heard the expression, "You are as old as you feel", well, there are some days we do feel old, which may only last a few hours or a day. As I said earlier, old is only a state of mind. If you think old, you will act old and gradually you will become an old person. I know how old I am, and that's enough. I act accordingly to how I think and feel, I think young so I feel young. I know my limitations, which is necessary to know as you age gracefully. Several measures are used to determine who is old. Chronological is the number of years a person has lived. Biological is a measure of a person's physical fitness. To be physically fit, our body parts should work well, meaning we are young biologically but old chronologically. A young person who is overweight and not able to run one hundred yards may be considered biologically old but chronologically young. So you see, age is a personal thing. Most young people think everybody is old. When you pass a certain age, it's really no special age you are just much older than they are. We thought the same way until we became those ages, now we consider those ages as young. We grew into a person from our parents. All living things share a common pattern: development, growth, aging, and death. Don't you wonder sometimes why we age and wish we could stop the process at the age or stage of life that we want to? The study about aging is called Gerontology. Not all signs of aging can be seen. Some changes take place inside a person's body during aging. Changes that take place inside a person's body are called internal changes. The part of the body where changes often occur is the heart and blood vessels. As a person ages, the heart may not be able to work as well as it once did, causing so many people to join exercising clubs or just walk, which is a good exercise. Research shows that people who follow healthy lifestyles when they are young are usually healthy when they are older. A happy and physically fit older person was probably a happy and physically fit young person. A sad or overweight older person was probably a sad and overweight young person. You have a responsibility to control your health. One of the best compliments an older person appreciates is "you don't look your age, you look much younger". You can improve your chances of a healthy aging if you practice some of the following behaviors: Have goals in life, think positively, learn to deal with stress, do not smoke, eat a well-balanced diet, participate in a planned schedule of physical activities, and you can add some personal things to the list that you can do to slow down the aging process. Love and treat yourself good.

Grandma

Etiquette

One of my grandma's friends called me because she was very upset. She is planning on having a shower for her great-grandbaby. Most of the people she invited had not responded (RSVP). When a RSVP is requested, please respond because this lets the host or hostess who are preparing for this occasion know who's planning to attend. Why people don't RSVP, I don't know. I question why they think it's on the invitation. A lot of us are guilty of this. I know I was at one time. I changed when I realized how important and the problem it can cause. Remembering when my cousin and I attended a 45th wedding anniversary dinner party. We were late because we couldn't find the hotel which was off the main road, and we kept missing the turn. We were an hour late trying to find the hotel. All the guests were there when we arrived, and we did not have a seat. But because we sent in our RSVP, they accommodated us. What happened was the young lady told us several people did not send them their RSVP causing them to add tables. This is not fair to the party giving the affair. People would have been mad or upset if they would have refused them on entering the affair. It doesn't take any time to do the right thing, and we should always respond to a RSVP. Take a minute and put yourself in that person's shoes. You are planning an affair for 50 people, but only 25 have RSVP'd. It is not the hostess place to contact these people to see if they are planning to attend. A hostess goes all out to make the affair a success. Because they have heard from 25 guests, they hostess has prepared for 30. Now here's what happened: All 25 of her non-responding guests show up. How do you think the hostess feels? I would say a little angry and disappointed that the guests did not RSVP. Not responding, you have caused her to prepare for less people and now she is wondering if she's going to have enough food and drinks for everyone. Do you see the situation you put her in? The hostess sets the tone for the occasion. It's important to keep him or her in good spirits. So next time you receive an invitation to RSVP please do.

Grandma

Planning a Trip?

Things don't happen just because you talk about what you want to do. It happens because you plan and put it into motion. You have to ask yourself some questions:

1. What – Type of trip you want to take?
2. Where – The place you want to go?
3. How – Transportation to get there?
4. Who – People involved?

A plan is like a road map, it guides you in the direction you want to go. Following your plan will help you to make changes if you have to. If you are not a good planner, you can always ask someone to do it for you. All you have to do is give them the necessary information they need to execute the plan. Planning a trip should be an exciting adventure. You might have to go on a shopping spree, depending on where you are planning to go or what you are planning to do. New clothes sometimes make you feel good, even though the old ones have everything to match them. Some people go on diets before they go on trips, especially when they plan to go on cruises. They know all about the food and how you can eat all day as much as you desire. That's why they diet so they won't have to worry about the pounds they gain. Food can be very expensive on some trips, especially eating three meals a day. I don't know whether being on a trip makes you hungry or it's just a habit of eating three meals a day. No matter what your trip costs it is well worth it. Getting away sometimes from your routine and environment is the best thing you can do for yourself. It relieves a lot of stress giving you time to think and cater to no one but you. It's a time when you're not on a schedule and can do anything you want to. I would think it's a time to be at peace with you. Some of us call our trips a vacation which gives us the freedom from school, business, home, or other duties. These moments are to be enjoyed to the fullest. After a vacation, you look and feel like a different person and you are ready to get back in the swing of things.

Grandma

Family History

One day I was thinking about family members who are no longer here on earth with us. We have new and younger members in our family whom have never seen them in person but know only of them when they hear a family member mention their name. I know at some family reunions they go way back in the family tree, but that's not what I'm talking about. I'm talking about the family members who recently passed on and the children were too young to know them. Whether we liked them or not, we should at least let our children know something about them. It could help them identify and learn something about these close relatives. The youngsters, depending on their age, may ask questions so be prepared.

Here's my family history that I would like to tell. I had two aunts, one name Rose who had 3 children, and the other named Addie. They lived in the same house, one upstairs and one downstairs. They were both very good cooks, but their cooking styles were different. Aunt Rose was a good ol' Georgia cook. Everything was prepared in a simple manner but was excellent in taste. Her fried chicken was in a category all by itself; it just melted in your mouth, juicy and good. Most of us can fry chicken but only a few had the magic touch like she did. Now her cakes were the same way, superior. She just dumped ingredients in the bowl and mixed. She was serious about her cooking and baking, and did not have much patience with me. She could tell I was not that interested in learning to bake. I only made one plain cake, and one coconut cake with her supervision. Thank God she has one granddaughter named Erica that carries out her legacy of cooking and baking in the family. Now, Aunt Addie, if she was living today, would be gourmet. Everything she made was in parts and had to be a certain quality. In her younger days, she had a restaurant. She could season and make one piece of meat taste like another. If you're from the south, you should know what I'm talking about. You never knew what you were eating, with Aunt Addie. She would tell you it was one thing, laugh, and in the end after you ate it, tell you what it really was that you were eating. She was a good cook too. I only ate what I knew I was eating. She also loved to make wine and preserves. And then there was Uncle Harry who came from Louisiana to come live with us when his brother, Aunt Rose's husband, died. Uncle Harry loved us and we loved him. He had a jolly personality and was the father figure in our family. Just tell the younger generation the outstanding things they did. If they want to know more, they will ask. Give them a reason to be proud of their family. What you think is not important to us, may be important to them, and it may also help them identify things about themselves. Since Thanksgiving is soon to come and the family will be together, this would be a good time to put the family history together and every year adds another family member.

Grandma

My Favorite Student: Don

My first teaching class in special education was what they called a "self-contained" class. This class consisted of mixed classifications. Each student was different and had to be treated as such. I had seven students. I not only taught them, but I counseled them too. First I let them know that I was their teacher, and that I cared about them, and the reason that they come to school is to learn and do all their class work, so that they can eventually return back to their regular class. In this class, some of the students were on mainstream for a regular class of math and reading, but because of their behavior, social skills and academic reinforcement, they had to remain in this class. The ages were 7-9, and very active students. There was one 9-year old student I will never forget, and I know he will never forget me. His name was Don. He was very smart, but had a serious behavior problem. One that he had to be escorted everywhere he went outside of the classroom, because he was so destructive. After assigning each student their class work, instead of sitting at my desk, I would sit at the table in the back of the classroom. There, I would talk with each student (one each day), and to make sure they were listening, I would ask a question on what I was talking about. I know sometimes when we talk; we sometimes don't hear each other. When talking to a younger person, find out what they like, and don't like. Talking with Don, I found out he liked math, and he liked using a calculator. During these times, calculators were only used to check answers. Don was the student that made me look good as a teacher. The whole school knew him, and he was already classified so it was not hard to label him as being "bad" or "destructive", and that's the way he behaved. I knew I had to correct his behaviour first. After talking and observing Don along with the other students, I noticed certain things about him. He was very smart, excellent in math, would finish his class work then would disturb the other students. I knew I had to solve this problem immediately, and this is what I did: The next day, I had Don stand in front of the class. I told the class that he was very smart and we were going to help him get back into his regular class, the class agreed. I also made him my helper, and well, that did it. That was the day of change. He gave us his cheesecake smile, and promised he would try to do better, which he did. When I met his parents, the first thing they told me was "Don said, that his teacher like him and that he was the class helper", this made him feel special, knowing that I, his teacher, cared, and being the teacher's helper gave him the attention he needed to eliminate being destructive. So you see how important it is for a student to know you care. They will try to do their best to please you. After weeks of improvement, I set up an appointment with the child's study team. I was ready to see him get the chance that he worked so hard for. He promised me he would do his best and he did. I was so proud of him. The teacher whose class he was going to, we had a working relationship, so she was willing to give him a chance. She made it very clear, if he acted up, he would have to return because she had a class of 26 students. Don made it through the last 6 weeks of school, and he was promoted. I was happy, he was happy, and his family was happy. That was my reward and the beginning of my teaching career. You give a lot when you're a teacher and you receive a lot in return because each class has many students, but one teacher.

Grandma

How Is Your Self-Esteem?

We are not born with self-esteem. Self-esteem comes from a lifetime of experiences. Family, home, environment, school work, and our social life all contribute to our self-esteem. Self-esteem is how we feel about ourselves when we look in the mirror. If affects every aspect of our lives, how we think, how we act and feel, and how we relate to others. Learning to feel good about ourselves can help overcome depression, stress and loneliness. If you want to create a positive self-esteem, look at your strengths. Building self- esteem takes action. Make a list of the things you do well, such as cooking, sewing, or playing a sport. List the reasons people like you. If you have trouble knowing, ask a family member or friend to help you out. Also, what you like about yourself. Next, we're going to identify our weaknesses. We all have strengths and weaknesses. Take a honest look at the things you don't like about yourself and identify things you would like to improve and the things you cannot change. Accepting yourself is the BEST change you can make. Focus on your good qualities. Use positive statements such as "I am strong", "I am lovable", "I am a good cook." Say and think about your affirmations until they feel like a part of you. Be around people who make you feel good about yourself, and avoid people who are negative or put you down. The better your relationships, the faster your self-esteem will rise. Try doing some things that help you feel good about yourself. Look at the list of things you do well for ideas. Try new things, take up a new hobby or make a new friend, or volunteer to help others. Each new positive experience will counter act an old negative experience. Don't expect perfection, everyone makes mistakes, even at the things we do well. Be your own best friend and take pride in what you do. Encourage and praise yourself, eat right, exercise, rest and play. Caring for yourself in these ways can boost your self-esteem. Picture yourself at your best. Keep that picture in your mind and then take action. At first take small easy steps toward change, then as your confidence grows tackle the hard changes. Remember to acknowledge every small step, focusing on improvement not perfection. Building your self-esteem should be all about ME, MYSELF and I. Doing these things; you will become the person you want to be.

Grandma

Woman's Conference

Last month, I attended a woman's conference in Albany. The title of the conference was "I'm Starting with the Woman in the Mirror". There were many women in attendance. Also, mirrors were displayed all around so you could look in the mirror if you chose to. Looking in the mirror naturally, you see yourself. Most of the time we judge our outside appearance as our total look, which is only one part. The other part of us is our inner, which cannot be seen but will show through our behavior and expressions. Have you ever seen a person act different than the way they look? In other words, on the outside they appear to be a nice, easy going person but their action was just the opposite of their look. They exhibit mean behavior and this behavior will surprise you. That's the side you can't see and a lot of us wear what we call a "mask." We pretend to be someone whom we are not thinking the hair, clothes, and make-up make a statement of who we are. There's nothing wrong with having a good appearance but it's not the only look we have. The inner part of us is the substance of our character. It shows the knowledge we have obtained in life. Both inner and outer is important for our development and growth. Therefore, we as individuals are responsible for our own growth. I've heard adults say "That's the way I am", or "I've always been this way and I can't change now". It's never too late to change for the better. Some people feel they're too old, whatever excuse you have is ONLY an excuse you use keeping you from obtaining your goal. These were the topics that the speaker spoke on: "Stop Whining and Start Smiling" and "Walking with Courage Down the Road of Life "and our discussion was "Let's Get into the Know." We broke up into groups of ten to write on charts that were all around the room. Our topic was "What was your idea of a good life?" These are some of the things written for a good life: less stress, good health, living peaceable with all people, love all, a happy family life, support our families in church, trusting in God's word, having money to pay our bills, having faith, wisdom, and patience, being successful, being saved, and a good marriage. Having all these things would make a good life. It was good to see so many beautiful women assembled together, sharing and being enriched at this conference.

Grandma

Friends and Acquaintances

Traveling along this life's journey, I've made a lot of friends and acquaintances. When I hear older people say they only have a few friends left because they either moved or died, my heart goes out to them. I've lost some of my old friends to, but I gained just as many new ones as I've traveled along in life. You can't just stay home and never visit outside of your environment. There's people, places, and things to see. I bet many of you never traveled alone. It might be a little scary at first, but if you try it you will realize that many people travel alone. Others cannot always travel or go places for whatever reasons with you. You will meet people who travel alone. There are many organizations that you can join, or just meet people on your own, that enjoy the same things you do. If you are or if you're not a people person read on. A people person is one who associates with all kinds of people. By the time they reach a certain age, they've met them all. The new people you meet may have a different name, but their character is the same. With so many people in the world, no one should be lonely or friendless. If you are, you should try to change it. As long as there is life, changes can be made. Knowing a person's character is a good thing. It saves you a lot of time and energy trying to find the person out. If you're not a people person, and now you feel all alone because your friends are few, when you were young you probably limited yourself to friendships and didn't bother with many people except your family. Living in a world of people, we need each other even if we think we don't. Our senior life should be enjoyed, along with the aches and pains. Some seniors need advice but won't take it. They just say, "I know" or give you excuses. They know that you're telling the truth but no changes are being made, that's why we should evaluate our lives on a yearly basis. This will help you be aware of things that are happening in your life or around you. It's never too late to make short term and long term goals, and good decisions when you have to. This will help avoid the lonely "trap" when you get older.

Grandma

Explaining and Complaining

One of my relatives from up north always calls to talk about some personal things that go on in her life. After talking with her on one occasion, she said, "I'm sorry for always complaining and thanks for listening, I feel much better now." My response to her was "You weren't complaining, you were just explaining what was bothering you." She said she never thought of it that way and liked the way I put it. Explaining, not complaining. Sometimes you have to explain a situation to get clarity on it, so that the person you're talking to can give you good wholesome feedback or just listen so that you can hear yourself and relieve some of the stress that it's causing. I know there are many of you who listen to your friends or family members complaining and explaining, and that's a good thing. If you think back, somebody listened to you explaining and complaining. There should always be someone in this world that you can talk to. All of us have something going on in our lives that we wish we could change, but we can't, so it might be our cross to bear. Praying, explaining, and complaining will make us feel better, even if the situation remains the same. Complaining is when we are dissatisfied and we find fault with the situation. Explaining is to make a clear picture and to explain the meaning of what is happening. It might be a little difficult at times to separate the two. Most people who talk a lot tend to explain and complain a lot. If a person of this nature complains constantly and you really don't want to hear it, I think you should tell that person in a nice way. If you can't tell them, then you should continue to listen in a nice way. Be aware, some people just like to vent and let out their feelings. Once that's done, they are on their merry way and you're left feeling sorry or bad about what they have told you. That's when you have to decide whether you are going to continue to listen or tell them you can't listen anymore, with or without a reason. Being a good listener is okay, if you're helping. You be the judge.

Grandma

Change

I don't know why people don't change knowing that they are unhappy with their present situation. I believe it's because they use the words "I can't change", or "I'm too old to change". You're never too old to change. If you say you can't change, you won't be able to. You can't change by yourself, you need help, and help comes from the Lord. To change is scary. Many people know what is at present but doesn't know what the future holds, in fact, none of us do. But those of us who try to live a positive life, and prepare ourselves for the future in case we live to see it think and plan what we would like to do or accomplish years to come. I remember years ago, sitting at my table, the questions came to mind "Are you content with your life at present?" "Do you want to be doing what you're doing ten years from now?" My answer was no. Another question came to mind, "What are you going to do about it?" That's when I realized, I must change things in order for change to take place. To be honest, I didn't know how to change. I think this situation happens to many of us. We want to change things, we just don't know how. This becomes such a personal thing that we can't share it with anyone because they just wouldn't understand our inner feelings. Remember, we are judged from the outer appearance and to them we seem to be okay. We know our situation appears good, but we also know how we feel. Something is getting ready to happen, we don't know what it is, but we just feel it. I call it a transition. When this is happening, who do we turn to? Nobody but Jesus, and he know how to get our attention. We pray and wait for our answers. When we pray for change, change will come, doors will open, God will put people in our path to help us on our way, and we will perform duties and exercise talents we didn't know we had.

This brings to mind the verse **Philippians 4:13**

King James Version:

I can do all things through Christ who strengthens me.

New Living Translation:

For I can do everything with the help of Christ who gives me the strength I need.

When we know and believe this, we are well on our way. It's never too late to make a change. Some of us are going to have a hard time changing and may never change because of our pride. It takes courage and faith to make changes. Courage is our mental ability to make changes without fear, and faith is our belief in God and his promise, so with that knowledge we can make our changes unfold and be thankful to God for blessing us as we change

Grandma

The Inner Voice

I often hear people say "God will see me through, he didn't bring me this far to leave me" and that is so true, but you must also help yourself. All of us have an inner voice. I say that is God speaking to us, especially when things lay heavily on our minds. When this happens, we should think about it, pray about it, and if we can, when the time is right, act upon it. When people speak, I listen. I hear clearly what they are saying. Most of them make excuses on why they are not doing what the inner voice is saying or what they would like to do. Opportunities do not knock every day, so we have to prepare ourselves to make things happen. Did you forget that you can do all things through Christ that strengthens you? How many times have you said this? I bet many. As the grandmothers would say, "Actions speak louder than words." Action is when you're doing something, and not just talking about it. You would be surprised how happy you would be trying something new. You know about the old things, new things; you continue to learn while you're on your life's journey. You know what is so sad, is when you talk to people and they tell you their story or part of the story of their lives and how they regret how they didn't do what they desired to do. In most cases, the opportunity had presented itself, and they really had no excuse, they just didn't want to do it and now they are expressing their regret. I bet we all know someone who has been in this situation and let their opportunity pass them by. The reason why I'm writing this is because I know there's probably someone experiencing hearing their inner voice, and doesn't know what to do, as I said before, always pray, and your answers will come. Sometimes we have to ask others for their advice. You will get negative and positive feedback. Think about both, their feedback may be something you didn't think about until they bought it to your attention and could be helpful when making your decision. If there's any way possible, talk to people who are doing what your inner voice is telling you to do. Remember, they have been where you are now and can give you constructive advice. Don't just rely on one person, talk to several because everyone's outlook is different. Also, if you can find a role model or a mentor, that will help tremendously. Ask, seek, and knock are the three keys that will open the door to a successful life.

Grandma

Water

To early man, water was alive. It was truly living water. It moved, made many sounds, as rain it pattered, in the brook, it tinkled and murmured. In the surf of the sea, it roared. Its power in storms and floods is evident. However, it is more helpful to us than harmful. It quenches our thirst, and we need it to survive. Some people say it has no value to the body other than to stop dehydration, but what about when it rains. It has different rain patterns. A drizzle is a sprinkling rain, a down pour is sometimes such a heavy rain that you can't see the car in front of you if you are driving. There are times we had to stop along the road until it slacked up or stopped. Again, in the brook, it twinkled like little sparkling diamonds. The waves of the ocean roar in on the beaches. Look at the power it has in storms, leaving areas flooded. The first thing that comes to mind about water is the water we drink. But, water is used for so many things like washing our clothes and bodies. I've heard we can survive longer with water than food and Evil spirits cannot cross running water or remain in it. As I continue to write about water, the more interesting it is to know how valuable water is to us. Have you ever had your water shut off for any reason? That's when you realize how high the usage of water is in your home. You would be surprised to know what goes on in the life of our water. It's a world in itself. We only see the top but there's a lot going on below the surface.

Grandma

Moving to a New State and City

If you are thinking about moving to another state and city, there are certain things you should consider before moving. Every city and state has its own personality and lifestyle. Visiting is one thing, living is another. You probably enjoyed your visit, and that's what motivated the idea of moving. You should take this move serious, and if you're a couple, both of you should agree to make this move. Here are several things to take into consideration before you decide to move: the type of weather, and if you can adjust properly to the weather. You might have been living in a cold climate, now the new state is hot most of the time. Also, because of the warm or hot weather, you have grass, trees, bushes, flowers, and bugs all year causing other problems. Another important thing to consider is what type of doctors and medical services are available to you and your family, and also the distance of a hospital, in case of an emergency, the type of housing, their price range, and locations. School is very important also, especially if you have children. You always want the best for them. Check out how many schools are available, in elementary, middle, and high schools and what they are teaching. Don't forget the daycares and head starts; include them because that is the beginning of a child's education. Colleges are also a plus too. Many young and older adults have become successful because of the availability of education from technical colleges universities in their state and town. There should be social and recreational functions also for the family. Children like to participate in sports and music. If you like to shop, look for a mall. Dining and restaurants may be another important motive for your idea of moving. Will you be able to go to a movie, see a show, or play sometime? What types of organizations are available to you? Maybe you're a member already and want to join up in the new town. There are so many things you must consider before moving. It is easy to move, but the question is will you be happy after moving? I know several people who moved and were unhappy because they considered none of the above. And, I know some that are happy because they did their homework and knew what to expect in their new environment. It does make a difference so check it out before you make the big move to see if it offers you a good lifestyle for you and your family.

Grandma

"Summer Soul Fest"
It Was Showtime at the Civic Center

Charlie Wilson, the Whispers, and T.K. Soul: What a Show! To those who did not attend, you missed a real treat. Folks were singing, dancing, and having a good time. I saw many happy and smiling faces. Sometimes you have to get out and have a little fun, no matter what the price is. Music is always good for the soul, and believe me, my soul is still rejoicing. I enjoyed the whole show. I admired Charlie Wilson and the Whispers and because they didn't forget who made them. Uncle Charlie, as he is also known, stated that he has always set aside time in his shows for God because he knows what he has done for him. He gave a beautiful testimony, it was a real testimony, and was thanking God for his journey, his ups and his downs, and what he's done, and what he's doing for him right now. Remember, he was the lead singer in the Gap Band, which had hits like "Party Train," "Yearning For Your Love," "I Don't Believe You Want To Get Up and Dance," "You Dropped a Bomb on Me," and many more. Now Charlie Wilson is a solo artist and he gave a dynamic show. When I saw the four girl dancers, I thought about James Brown and his dancers. Uncle Charlie entertained us. He had us rocking, singing, and dancing. His special light scene was awesome! This was the first time I saw a lighting scene, you would have had to be there to know what I'm talking about. T.K. Soul set the tone, and got the crowd in the mood to party. The Whispers, when they hit stage singing all their hit records, took me down memory lane, and the sound was great. This was my first time seeing them in person, having all their records and albums back in the day. We didn't have CDs back then; we had records which sounded good. At the show, their sound put me in a trance. They sounded better today than 50 years ago, maybe because they were in person. We rocked right along with them as they rocked on stage singing "And the beat goes on," "Rock Steady," and many more. When Nickolus Caldwell told his story about his audition for the Whispers, and the song he wrote ("Lady"), it touched my heart. For the moment I was in love. Oh, I almost forgot, the Whispers, like Uncle Charlie, were grateful to God for the years he had given them. He gave them 50 years in the music business. It's wonderful when God has blessed you, and you are thankful. To the promoters of the Summer Soul Fest, thank you, and please continue to bring the best entertainment to Albany.

Grandma

Shop at a Boutique

Since I've arrived in Albany, Georgia many new businesses have come to town such as eateries, hotels, pet shops and lady boutiques. I got into a discussion with a friend about fashion trends in reference to the boutiques that were in town. A boutique is usually a small shop that specializes in stylish clothes and accessories especially designed for women. The professionals that own these boutiques are not only fashion icons but fashion consultants. Garments are handpicked for their clients to enhance their individual attributes. All women are beautiful and want to feel special. Shopping in a boutique has its advantages because you can develop a personal relationship. Men can also shop at a boutique for their mothers, wives and significant others for all occasions. Men need to know that we ladies do not like household products on our special days we want something just for us. So if you have a problem shopping in a department store, a boutique is for you. Look around town and I'm sure you will find one. Just make sure you know your ladies size she might not want to tell you. All you have to do is look in her closet and find the label that states the size. After you have picked out the garment you can accessorize them with the jewelry, hand bags, belts or scarfs.

Shopping for your lady should be on your list of things to do.

Grandma

Peace

I believe if you live right, love God, self, and your fellow man, you will be able to enjoy peace in your life. You should treat people the way you want to be treated. To reach this point requires some discipline, making right choices in your decision, and even sacrificing things that you would like to do. Another thing that can rob you of your peace is letting other people burden you with their problems. They can only do this if you let them. Sometimes it's hard to say no, but that is the decision you have to make in order to keep your peace. When a person becomes an adult, they are responsible for their own life. They will always make excuses and blame others for whatever is happening with them. They will not have peace with all their problems because peace is a state of quietness, and a calm spirit. Like I said, don't let others, including your children rob you of your peace by letting their problems be your problems. Remind them that they made the decision or choice that causes the situation that they are in. Refer them to Romans 14: 11-12: King James Version: [11]"For it is written as I live" said the Lord, "Every knee shall bow to me and every tongue shall confess to God" [12]So then every one of us shall give account of himself.

New Living Translation

[11]For the scriptures say, "As surely as I live" says the Lord, "Every knee will bow to me, and every tongue will confess allegiance to God." [12]Yes, each of us will have to give a personal account to God. When we are peaceful, we will have a calm spirit. We will see things with our spiritual eyes, judging not, but embracing love, happiness, and peace. These are the main things in life that we should strive for, along with our other goals. In my opinion, each one of us is responsible for our own lives, so pray and protect your life at all times.

Grandma

What Is Your Calling?

Did you know a calling is a profession? I know some of us think a calling is only to a ministry. For years, I thought that too until I looked up the word in the dictionary. It stated that it was an occupation, profession, or trade. An occupation, profession, and trade requires years of academic studies and internships. Most of these occupations, professions, and trades, when completed, will serve the public in some kind of way. Many of us have worked in one of these capacities without realizing it was a calling and that's why we are so dedicated. Those of us that were dedicated and committed to our professions did more than what was required of us because we had a passion about what we were doing. Teachers are just not people that teach your children, they endure many roles during their years of teaching, such as a parent, counselor, nurse, or whatever a child's needs are when they are in the teacher's care. If you ever been in the hospital as a patient, you can always tell the medical people who are passionate about their job. They are patient, kind, and will make you comfortable while you are in the hospital. Now, the doctors always seem to be in a hurry, I guess that's because they have so many patients in the hospital, they are on tight schedule and they have to rush. We want them to know patient care is important to us, and they should give us the best of care. Your health is very important, and so is your healthcare provider. Occupation and trades are very important callings also. Chefs provide the delicious meals that we eat at restaurants, hair stylists and barbers provide us with hair care, and car salesman and mechanics maintain our cars. We have every type of services provided for us to meet all our needs. In most cases, you will have to be educated in your profession, occupation, and trade. Find the school where you can learn your calling and you will be rewarded in the end for accepting your calling.

Grandma

A Time for Everything

Time is one of the most valuable and important things we have. Time is measured in years, months, weeks, days; everything is based on time, as it written in

Ecclesiastes, 3rd chapter: verses 1-8,
King James Version.

[1]To everything there is a season, and a time to every purpose under the heaven. [2]A time to be born, and a time to die; a time to plant and a time to pluck up that which is planted. [3]A time to kill, and a time to heal; a time to break down, and a time to build up; [4]A time to weep, and a time to laugh; a time to mourn and a time to dance; [5]A time to cast away stones, and a time to gather stones together; a time to embrace, and a time to refrain from embracing. [6]A time to get, and a time to lose; a time to keep, and a time to cast away; [7]A time to rend, and time to sew; a time to keep silence, and a time to speak. [8]A time to love, and a time to hate; a time of war, and a time of peace.

Ecclesiastes, 3rd chapter: verses 1-8,
New Living Translation

[1]There is a time for everything; a season for every activity under heaven. [2]A time to be born and a time to die; a time to plant and a time to harvest.

[3]A time to kill and a time to heal; a time to tear down and a time to rebuild. [4]A time to cry and a time to laugh; a time to grieve and a time to dance.

[5]A time to scatter stones and a time to gather stones; a time to embrace and a time to turn away. [6]A time to search and a

time to lose; a time to keep and a time to throw away.
⁷A time to tear and a time to mend; a time to be quiet and a time to speak up. ⁸A time to love and a time to hate; a time for war and a time for peace.

So I concluded that there is nothing better for people than to be happy and enjoy themselves as long as they can. People should eat, drink and enjoy the fruits of their labor, for these are the gifts from God.

Grandma

A Gift of Love; a Plant

Some Gifts should mean just as much to the giver as it does to the person receiving the gift especially, if it's someone you care or think a lot of. Mother's Day, Anniversaries, Christmas, Easter and Birthdays are special Days. Year after year we give gifts to those we love on those special days. I remember the gift I gave to my Aunt Rose; it was a big beautiful Hanging plant. It was so green and shiny it looked real. I thought of this fantastic idea because the live plants would only last for a short period of time where as this plant would last as long as you wanted to keep it. My logic was not always understood, but it worked. Auntie hung that plant in her living room between the windows the same as if it was a living plant. It hung there year after year as long as she lived. In fact it was the only plant in the living room. You can call me an "Indian Giver" if you want because I did asked the family for the plant back. Naturally they said yes! Today the beautiful plant has traveled from New Jersey to Georgia and is the center piece on my Coffee table. I named it Rose a gift of love that was returned to me in the memory of my Auntie Rose.

Grandma

Storm Sandy

I said I wasn't going to write about the storm, but I had to say a little about Sandy. I'm not going into a lot of detail because we all knew what happened. I said God stepped in to remind us of who is in charge. We can say whatever we want to say, but those who know the power of God know. Some people think strange things are happening; No, it's the power of God. Here's how I know: he didn't let the storm Sandy happen in a familiar area because people would have thought it was just another storm. He sent it up north where they don't have these types of storms, and look what it did, stopped everything! It put people in darkness, flooded areas, tunnels, and subways, and caused fires and sandy streets. Something happened that never happened before in the Northeast. We as people sometimes act very foolish and not godly as we should. We better stop, take a good look at ourselves and stop playing. My prayers are with the people who lost everything. In fact, I prayed for everybody. It is praying time people because God is not through with us yet. The storm brought people together. It softened and humbled hearts. God showed us on national television what he can do. As I watched the many things that were happening, my thoughts were: how can a person doubt and not serve a mighty God? The news people were speaking about New Jersey and New York and what had been going on there. I always hear New York is the city that never sleeps. As the news man was speaking, he said "The city that never sleeps will sleep tonight" because they had no electricity. Just imagine a busy city like New York being shut down and in darkness and powerless. What does that tell you? It tells you that man is limited and can only do what God allows him/her to do. Sandy did a lot of damage in a short time. Sometimes when strange things happen they wonder why. I'm a believer that things happen for a reason. We don't always know the reason, we just know what happened. But, as the old folks would say, "Just keep on living and you'll understand it all by and by". Disasters bring people together allowing them to become human beings again, even if it's for the moment. The things we take for granted becomes a necessity for our survival. What really takes place is a reality check causing us to realize we're all God's children, no matter what our color is: red, yellow, black, or white, we are ALL precious in his sight. The sooner people realize and believe this, the better we as a people will be.

Grandma

Happy Holidays

Happy holidays to all. The true meaning of our holidays is the birth of Christ. Over the years, it has become so commercial that the joyful spirit is gone. People are spending money they don't have. What happened to the dinners and family gatherings? There are probably still a few families enjoying the old fashion way of celebrating the holidays, but there are so many of us who are guilty of big spending. We buy gifts for people, giving them things they really don't need. Now they have gifts cards, so a person can purchase whatever they want. That may be good for the young people who like to choose their own gifts, but some older people are just happy to be living and really don't mind if they receive a gift or not, but there are exceptions. We still have some people who like gifts. If you don't know what to buy, or maybe you're a person who doesn't like to shop, going in and out of stores is not your thing. I truly understand because I, myself am like that. Money is the answer. Everybody's happy to receive money, especially the kids. Give it to them and watch their face light up like Christmas trees. It's not the amount that matters but the thought of giving. Years ago people seemed to be excited about the holiday approaching. Now, because it's so commercial, some people dread the holidays. And some act as if it's just another day. However we should feel it is a time to celebrate, starting with the birth of Christ. The greatest gift should be love. Love costs nothing, and can be given away freely. If everyone would give love, this world would be a better world. We can't change the world but we can change ourselves, causing the world to change. Some people are sad when the holidays come because of their lives change so much in most cases for the worst instead of the better. If they would look at their situation with a positive outlook, they would see positive things instead of negative things. It's not what happens; it's how you view your situation. No matter what happens, you should try to see the brighter side. There are so many things you can do. I was telling a friend that I visit the nursing home on Tuesday and go some Thursdays to the children's daycare, as a volunteer. I could not believe that she said that I must be bored to do that. I told her I was not bored, and was passionate about what I was doing. Babies and old folks have something in common, they're just happy that you pay them some attention. On Tuesdays at the nursing home, they play bingo. I sit with those who need help finding the numbers. Last Tuesday, one of my ladies whom I was helping had black out, covering the whole board. She was so happy. To be a part of someone else's happiness makes you feel good. It's the little things that matter. The children are the same way; they just want your attention. To my understanding, boredom comes from doing nothing. Whenever you do something for someone else from your heart, it's a blessing. Think about this: it could be you in the nursing home, instead of you visiting as a volunteer. Also, everybody in the nursing home is not old. Visit sometimes and you will see how blessed you are. Again, Happy Holidays!

Grandma

A New Year

As we begin our new year, let's stop and review the old year, of the things we did and things we wanted to do but didn't do them. Don't make promises that you're not going to keep. Get a piece of paper, fold it in half, write "Things I Did Different" (not every day routines), examples: bought a car, moved, enrolled in school, took a trip, joined the church, etc. On the other side write "Things I Would like to Accomplish", when you're finished, put your paper in an envelope, say a little prayer and put it in a safe place. You can always add to your list when things pop into your mind. You will review it at the end of the year and you will be surprised of what you will accomplish at the end of the New Year. This is a good way of moving your life forward and knowing what you're doing. It's keeping inventory of you, which is good. We should not just go through life aimlessly, we should always be aware of what we're doing and why we're doing it and what is happening around us. You've heard the expression "Life is what you make it", some of that is true. Sometimes we do things, not always knowing why, that's when we use the expression "God only knows". In a lot of cases, he is the only one that knows, we can be lead and guided in the right direction if we humble ourselves. Life seems so complicated at times, but it's really simple. We complicate it by doing what we think we know. We should always have more than one plan to accomplish something. Keep trying until we succeed, or accomplish what we're trying to achieve. Failing doesn't mean you're a failure. Because you want something doesn't mean it's right for you. Failure sometimes means there is something better in store for you. Like I just said, just because we want it doesn't mean its right for us. Lord knows many things I wanted and when I got them, I wished I never had them. You know when you pray for something and you get it, you're so happy? Just wait, misery is on its way. After that, you become very careful of what you ask for. He will give you the desires of your heart.

Life teaches us so much. Why couldn't we have known what we know now when we were young? Well, I guess it wasn't meant to be. When I used to ask questions, no one would give me answers. Maybe they just didn't know how to answer them. That's the conclusion I came to after talking with an aunt of mine. She said I was always talking and asking questions.

Grandma

Your Cross to Bear

It seems like when we reach a certain age; we all have something going on medically. Don't let it get you down, pick yourself up and say "This is my cross to bear, and I am going to bear it." Name it, but don't claim it. Have you ever talked to a person, and by the time they finish telling you all that is wrong with them, it makes you feel almost as if nothing is wrong with you. You feel that your ailment is a big deal because it's yours. But when you hear someone else's story, yours is not that bad after all. No matter what's wrong, you're going to live. Whatever we are required to do, we must do. Eliminate doing things that are against you, such as drinking and eating the wrong foods. When you are diagnosed with a certain ailment, you are usually given material to read. If not, ask your doctor for it. You should be knowledgeable about your ailment and the medicines you are taking. Remember, your doctor has many patients, and you are just one amongst the many. It's not that he doesn't know or care about you, but you must care and show interest in yourself. We have a lot of good doctors in Georgia and they are ready to serve you. No matter what your circumstances are, they specialize. They will take many tests until they find out what is wrong. Many of us are afraid to know what's wrong, that's why we don't ask. It's better to know than not to know. A lot of illnesses are not as bad as they sound or seem. It's just the medical terms that scare you. We should educate ourselves about our condition and know for ourselves what we are doing medically. There is no need to be afraid; we can live with our condition. Many people have conditions that you won't believe, but they won't let it consume them. They do all the things they want to do in moderation. They have learned to control their condition, and live life to the best of their ability, while others let theirs consume them with limitations. It just seems like everyone's taking medicine these days. Keep check on your medicine and make sure it is helping you bear your cross.

Grandma

The Old Church

A charge to keep, a God to glorify who gave his son my soul to save and fitted for the sky. Every now and then, I have to go back, that's why it's good to never forget where you came from. It will keep you balanced. I was raised in the church, Union Baptist was the name. I remember how we had to sit on the front row of the church. If you talked, laughed, or chewed gum, any adult could reprimand you. All they had to do was look at you, and you knew you had to stop whatever you were doing. We were happy to be in church, that is when we saw many of our friends, and we also had a chance to participate in church activities. In most of our families, we had ministers, deacons, deaconess, ushers, and choir members. As I can remember, that was the basic of the church, no clubs. My grandmother was an usher, and she was a proud usher. I remember watching her wash, starch, and iron her uniform, and she was always on time when the church door opened. She was right there at her post. Of course, I was right by her side, entering the church. I went to the front, sat down, and watched others arrive. The deacons led the devotional service, singing common meter hymns and praying. Women participated also, singing, praying, and moaning "Lord have mercy!" There were no church programs, but you knew the order of service because it was the same every Sunday. After devotion, the choir would march in, sometimes with music, and sometimes without. They had a director and musician, who played the piano. The choir could really sing and they knew it. It seemed like more people shouted in the spirit back in the day, when the minister preached and the choir sang than they do today.

One Sunday, nine of us children joined the church, and we all got baptized at the same time. I was nine years old; most of us were around the same age, give or take an age or two. Why we all joined at the same time, I don't know, but it felt good. The church did a lot of good things with the youth. I remember the speeches and plays that I was a part of. I loved participating in church activities; it gave you a sense of pride as a young person. You weren't allowed to talk in church; you paid attention to what was going on. I didn't always understand the messages the preachers preached, but I did learn a lot in Sunday school, because you could ask questions. Our Sunday school teacher would explain our questions to us. I remember asking a question as a youngster, about Joseph, Mary, baby Jesus, and the heavenly Father. Well, I didn't understand how Jesus had two fathers, I just didn't understand. Knowing me, I probably asked too many questions, which annoyed my Sunday school teacher. She said I was fresh, that was the terminology she used. I wasn't fresh; I just didn't understand how Jesus had two fathers. It's funny how you can remember certain things that have happened so many years ago. I will never forget that, because my Sunday school teacher hurt my feelings. We didn't know things that the children know today. Asking too many questions back then, was a no no. Whatever an adult said right or wrong, you had to respect it. That's the way it was back in the day. They raised us good, the best way they knew how. Some of these children today need to be raised the old fashion way. Look how good we turned out, not bragging, but I'm glad I was raised the old fashion way.

Grandma

The Faucet of Love

Years ago, I attend a bible study class. It was different from the ordinary bible study. It was based on sharing. That's when I first realized that sharing may help a person who feels the same way that you do or similar. I don't remember what our topic was, but I do remember what I said. It might not have been a topic because I usually remember. I know each person had something to say. I spoke about love, and the way I felt about it. At the time, I, being a divorced woman, described love as being a water faucet that you can't shut on or off as you please. You may think you don't love that person because you shut off the faucet, but deep down within, love is still flowing. We might not admit this, but if we do some soul searching, we will say that's true. If you truly loved someone, you still love them. You might not be able to change the situation and sometimes the person will never know, but as long as you can forgive them in your heart, it will make you feel better. Time heals all wounds. After all, you did spend many years together, which contributed to your growth. If you look at it positively, you will see all the good that you shared in the relationship. In most cases, I bet it was better than anything else. We were young, vibrant, and learning. We made a lot of mistakes, and we learned from our mistakes which made some of us a better person. When I finished speaking, a young man said he had never thought of love as a faucet, and that made him understand what was going on with him. He didn't speak on his situation, but I bet his love was flowing again. After the meeting, he told me he didn't realize he still loved the person, that's all he said. Guess what, I know a couple who remarried after being separated for years, and they are still together, happily married. We don't always know what life has in store for us. Being stubborn only keeps us in a miserable state. Letting go and letting God fill our spirit with love will lead us to a happy life.

Grandma

Living Alone and Lonely

I wrote an article on living alone and not lonely, now this one is titled "Living Alone and Lonely." Most people that live alone and are lonely did not plan or prepare to be alone. It happened, leaving them totally unprepared. In most cases, this takes place when one of the person's divorces, dies, or just leaves the marriage or relationship that they are in and the other person did not think or prepare their selves for living alone. In most cases, the couple did everything together and the companionship is missed. I know people who live alone, male and female, that are lonely and I know people that are in relationships that are lonely also. I know you're wondering how the latter could be. It's because they didn't keep the relationship alive. You have to put something in the relationship in order to get something out of it. A relationship can do nothing itself without your input. Communication is so important. You should talk about things that are meaningful. Express yourself in a tactful way. The reason I think that some people don't like to talk because they feel it will end in an argument or the other person just won't understand what they are trying to say. Here's what I see and hear a lot of: people complaining and explaining their situation to people who in no way can help them. I don't mean when you are seeking honest advice, I mean the people who tell you the same thing over and over. Why can't they tell the person or people that are involved in the situation? Maybe if the person or people knew how you felt, they would help correct the situation, since it is them that are involved. Back to communication, and why I feel it's so important to talk. I can hear you saying "What are we going to talk about?" Talk about what you know is the person's greatest interest, even if it's not yours. It will open the door and lead you into other conversations. You should set aside time just to talk, and little by little you may work up to expressing yourself depending on how skillful you are when you talk. Another thing, start doing things together that involves the both of you. Like I said before, and I'll say it again, with so many people in the world, no one should be lonely. Change your routine, your habits, be honest, and become the person you really want to be. Don't be afraid of change, it will only help you out of being lonely, and maybe one day you will no longer be alone and lonely.

Grandma

Living Alone and Not Lonely

Everyone who lives alone is not lonely. In most cases, they are the happiest people because they do live alone. It is their choice to live alone. I'm not talking about the young people who are searching for a mate; I'm talking about the ones who have experience sharing their lives with others. Most of us are head of households and have been for years. We've been married, divorced, widowed, common lawed, or whatever. What I'm saying is, we've been there and have done that and know what it's all about living with another person. We have good days and bad days, whichever one out weights the other made our choice of living alone. The key to this lifestyle is loving you. When you love yourself, you can do so many enjoyable and wonderful things. Did you forget that you were born by yourself and will one day die by yourself? We're really like butterflies, we can fly all around by ourselves, and doing all the things we desire to do, being free to be you and make your own decisions. I have nothing against people who want to have a mate. I think it's great if that's what they want. But, they have to see the other side of the coin too. Living alone is peaceful and when you are peaceful, you are happy. When you are happy you are loveable, and when you are loveable, you enjoy life. Everything is real and meaningful to you. Doing nothing is sometimes the greatest pleasure. There are so many things you can do when you live alone. Loving and enjoying yourself takes priority. You can have many friendships. You are free to openly meet people in your travels and in most cases your home environment is your castle. The reason I am writing about this living alone and not lonely subject is because I know a lot of people think you're lonely when you live alone and that's not true.

It's hard to explain this to someone who is not in your shoes. They just don't understand and they fear what you're enjoying. You can be lonely with people all around you. The thing that I came to realize is as we mature, we change in our thinking. A lot of things that were important in younger years got less important as we moved on. In other words, we changed. Our mates do not always see, think, or feel the same way we do. And it can also be the other way around. We do not see, think, or feel the same about an issue at hand as they do. That's when communication is important. We must talk about the things that lay heavily on our hearts and minds. Do you notice that people really don't like to talk to each other? I'm talking about mates. They will talk to everybody but the person they should be talking to and that's what causes the real problem, no communication. Communication is one of the most important factors in the relationship. You must talk. I believe that a lot of relationships could have been saved if people were willing to talk. People are so emotional at this stage; screaming, yelling, or saying nothing does not solve the problem. This situation leads many people into living alone. Some survive and become happy campers and some because of their stubbornness, blaming everyone but themselves, lose out. We're not taught how to live together; we learn how to live together.

Grandma

Dogs – Madison, Dimples, Prince, and Rex

My neighbor has the two most adorable grand's, which she keeps occasionally. I laugh because these grand's are dogs, Madison and Dimples. They are cousins belonging to two sisters. Dimples and Madison are little girl dogs. Madison is very pretty, dainty and lady like. She's poised and wears the cutest outfits. She has a calm spirit. Now on the other hand, Dimples is just the opposite; a little tomboy with beautiful eyes. You would think she's the baddest little dog in the world because she's a barker. As long as I know the dog doesn't bite, I know how to make friends. After they calm down barking, you have to ignore them because they are curious about you in their space. Off and on, they will continue to bark at you. If they come close enough to smell you and let you pet them, be gentle and don't scare them. Only do this if the tail is wagging because that's a sign of a friendly dog. Well, Dimples and I have finally become friends. She lets me pet her now and doesn't bark at me as much as she used to. She's a cute little thing. Dogs have a lot of sense. I have raised several dogs; in fact, I have one now named Prince. He's spoiled and likes a lot of attention, which he gets. Everyone that knows him likes him and thinks he's a beautiful dog. He's an excellent house dog and protects the house at all times. Prince has a bark that will scare anybody. Now I have a real dog story to tell about a New Jersey dog named Rex. Rex was a beautiful German Sheppard dog. He belonged to my neighbors in New Jersey which was a couple houses up the street. They kept him chained in the back yard. Most of us in the neighborhood knew him. He would break loose from his chain when he was ready but would always return back in his yard. After some time had passed, Rex began to look neglected and we noticed the family was not at home. It appeared that Rex was left all alone. They left him with a pail of water. We, the neighbors began to feed Rex. One day I remember seeing him lying in the snow. Where he was laying had turned to ice. I took some carpet padding and laid it where Rex would lay at. Rex did survive the winter. One Saturday during the spring, my neighbor informed me that the animal control (dog catchers) was coming to get Rex. Do you know what this dog did? That's why I know dogs have a lot of sense. I was getting out of my car that day. I didn't see Rex. He jumped in my arms. When he stood up, he was as tall as I was. It scared me a little because his front legs were on my shoulders. He licked my face, got down, and headed back to his yard. I was a little shaken because it happened so fast but when I thought about it, this dog was thanking me for the food and water that I had given him. It was just an amazing experience I will never forget. I hope someone adopted him because he was a fine looking German Sheppard dog.

Grandma

"Children"

I hear so many people speak on how bad the children are today, like it's their entire fault. There are many things that contribute to their behavior. I think it's so unfair to just blame the children, especially in our world today. Remember the old saying, "Spare the rod, and spoil the child" you know what the rod was back in the day, the hand, shoe, belt, and don't forget the switches. I remember an aunt of mine complimented me on how a fine young lady I became. I thanked her and said, "With all the whooping I got, how can I be anything but." I was a child that always had to have the last word and you know old folks didn't play that. They believed a child should remain in a child's place. Today, children say anything and think its okay, but it's not. Some homes are not teaching like they used to. Manners and respect is a home teaching, you have to start teaching these babies very early. They enter the world smart and ready to control you, I observe them. Look into their little eyes and listen to their cry, and I bet you know what they want and they can't even talk. That alone should tell you something about their character. I learned a lot working with young children. Most of them are mirrors of their home and environment. Talking with them, you learn a lot about them. They are open and honest and will talk freely about what goes on in their lives. A lot of them lack the love and discipline they need. There is a certain mannerism that should be taught at a very young age. You can tell the child has been taught manners and respect by their actions, it shows what they know. I just don't like children being labeled as bad. Whenever someone says that, I respond "They are not bad, they are different." If you continue to label a child as being bad, that's all they will be because that's all they hear. But If you find something kind or good to say to them continually, it will bring a smile to their face and in time it will change their personality. Let's face it; no one likes to hear bad stuff all the time. Good remarks lift your spirits. Don't just tell the good child their good; tell the bad (different) child their good too, even if they're not. Teach and show them right from wrong and in due time you will see a difference in this child. They won't know if we don't teach them.

Grandma

The Word: 23rd Psalm

This is one of my favorite Psalms in the bible, and I know it is many of yours too. We can write about many things but it's nothing like writing about something that has helped and healed us. I call this Psalm my prescription. It has healed me on many occasions. I would say it 3 times a day, morning, noon, and night, and in between times if needed. It's a personal psalm, and I like how it starts off.

King James Version

[1]The Lord is MY Sheppard, I shall not want.

[2]He maketh ME to lie down in green pastures; He leadeth ME beside the still waters. [3]He restoreth MY soul; He leadeth ME in the path of righteousness for his name's sake.

[4]Yea though I walk through the valley of the shadow of death, I will fear no evil; For thou art with ME. Thy rod and thy staff, they comfort ME. [5]Thy prepares a table before ME in the presence of mine enemies. Thy anoints MY head with oil. MY cup runneth over.

[6]Surely goodness and mercy shall follow ME all the days of MY life and I will dwell in the house of the Lord.

New Living Translation

[1]The Lord is MY Sheppard, I have everything I need.

[2]He lets ME rest in green meadows; he leads ME beside the peaceful streams. [3]He renews MY strength; He guides ME along right paths, bringing honor to his name. [4]Even when I walk through the dark valley of death, I will not be afraid, for you are close beside ME. Your rod and your staff protect and

comfort me.

⁵You prepare a feast for ME in the presence of MY enemies. You welcome ME as a guest, anointing MY head with oil. MY cup overflows with blessings. ⁶Surely your goodness and unfailing love will pursue ME all the days of MY life and I will live in the house of the Lord forever.

This is one of the most effective Psalms in the Bible. There's healing power in this psalm. Young people, take my advice and let this psalm be your prescription when you're stressed, or just don't feel good. You will see how much better you will feel when you say it. Older grandmothers know this and want to pass it on to you so your spirits can be lifted. I thank God each and every day for the word.

Grandma

CARICHE'

Cariche' is a combination
Of my Grandparent names

Carrie & Richard

CARICHE'

Joined at the R

And the E' is me (Cynthia)

About the Author

Cynthia Cariche' Carter is a retired teacher from Paterson, New Jersey. In addition to her teaching assignments she was also a career counselor for Ramapo College, Mahwah, New Jersey and Passaic County. Upon moving to Albany, GA she became a substitute teacher for Dougherty County School System, Lee County School System, and Baby World Day Care. A staff member of the Civil Rights Institute and a Journalist for the Southwest Georgian newspaper. Most of all Grandma is a born again Christian and loves the Lord!

Contact Information

My name is Cynthia Cariche' Carter and I am the author of the Book *Ask Grandma?*

Some of the titles in my book might be helpful topics for women to discuss and if so I can be contacted by email: grandma.cariche@gmail.com and for personal inquires:

Cynthia Cariche' Carter
P.O. Box 70531
Albany Georgia 31708

www.ingramcontent.com/pod-product-compliance
Lightning Source LLC
Chambersburg PA
CBHW071453070426
42452CB00039B/1196